How to Outsell the Born Salesman

How to Outsell
the Born Salesman

WILLIAM W. FRANK

CHARLES L. LAPP

COLLIER BOOKS

A Division of Macmillan Publishing Co., Inc.

NEW YORK

COLLIER MACMILLAN PUBLISHERS

LONDON

How the Book Came to Be Written

AT THE start of my sales career in 1932 I became interested in learning successful selling techniques. I have since endeavored to assemble successful sales practices, not only from my own experience but also from books and lectures on salesmanship, sales clinics, sales meetings, and discussions with other salesmen about how and why they made or lost sales. Every suggestion made in this book, regardless of its source, has been tested by Charles Lapp or me and also by salesmen under our direction.

WILLIAM W. FRANK

LIKE Bill Frank, I am interested both in actual sales work and research into the methods of selling.

Early in my career I sold advertising, shoes, vacuum cleaners, and hosiery. For several summers I worked as a traveling representative for Drake University. During the last eight years I have been a professor of salesmanship and have traveled as a consultant for various companies, doing sales work and evaluating the techniques of other salesmen.

Both Bill Frank and I have been devoted to the idea of preparing a book which would really tell salesmen how to sell. Our ideas being similar, collaboration was the natural result. Preparing this book has been a pleasurable experience for both of us. We can only hope that *How to Outsell the Born Salesman* will prove to be as useful to salesmen as we intended it to be.

CHARLES L. LAPP

How the Book Can Be of Greatest Help to You

To GAIN the greatest benefit from this book, the authors suggest that you read only a few pages at a sitting, but reread and digest those pages until each idea becomes a part of you. Think about as many of your lost sales as possible, and compare what you did with the principles given in the book to see where you might have fallen down. Go over the standard sales story of your product or service and see if the ideas found in the book have been used in it. Listen to other salesmen talk about the sales they have made or lost, and thus profit by their experience. And as you do so, check yourself to see how many of the suggestions you have absorbed. Then practice, *practice*, and PRACTICE.

The sales-interview conversations between salesman and buyer throughout this book may not always represent what *you* would have said. However, remember that these are actual recorded sales interviews. They are somewhat shortened to make them easier for you to read, but all their thought-provoking value is left intact for you. When trying any of these sales strategies, always adapt them to your own personality, your own product or service, and the prospect to whom you are making the sales presentation. The best way to improve yourself is to evaluate each customer's reaction to your sales presentation.

Reading this book can't *make* you outsell the born salesman. But it *can* give you directions for improving as you practice. Remember, you must practice and practice these proved selling techniques until they become a fundamental part of your sales personality.

Acknowledgments

THE AUTHORS would like to thank their wives, Mrs. William W. Frank and Mrs. Charles L. Lapp, for their understanding cooperation while this book was being written. The authors are particularly indebted to Mr. Larry Spence, of Typhoon Air Conditioning, and Mr. William F. Bimson, of Wear-Ever Aluminum, who read the manuscript and made suggestions; and to Mrs. Adeline Verbarg, of Washington University, who edited and typed the final manuscript.

Contents

PART I

HOW TO APPLY FUNDAMENTALS TO YOUR SALES EFFORT

Chapter 1

Making Selling Pay Off For You

> Control your **appearance**
> Develop your **personality**
> Know the **what** and **why** of selling
> Memorize the **outline** of a **sale**
> Be **proud** you're a salesman

A MAN with exceptional social grace and self-confidence sometimes takes a job as a salesman. Operating largely by instinct, hunch, and habit, not knowing exactly the how or the why of his selling method, this man achieves some sales successes on the basis of his natural attributes. He is commonly referred to as the "born salesman." The born salesman depends on his natural attributes and those acquired by no definite program of self-improvement.

Outselling the Born Salesman

A gift such as commanding height or an attractive physique can be a wonderful asset to a salesman. However, it has been repeatedly proved that persons who rely on such gifts alone are no match for the dedicated students of sales techniques and strategy who strive by a planned program to improve themselves. In fact, if the salesman develops his "plus" assets and abilities, any physical shortcoming either is forgotten by prospects or becomes a useful identifying characteristic.

Salesmen gifted with naturally attractive features too often fail to improve because of their failure to look at their selling practices scientifically. One difficulty with the born salesman is that he fails to analyze weaknesses and strengths in his sales performance, so he does not know what to avoid or repeat in the future. Therefore, to improve yourself as a salesman your first step should be a desire to self-analyze.

Those aspects of yourself over which you have control are far more important to your success as a salesman than the mannerisms and characteristics with which you were born. Natural gifts are unimportant compared to what you can achieve through study and practice. With the proper attitudes you soon develop the effective abilities.

Outstanding Salesmen Are Self-Made

In fact, the outstanding salesman is probably more a self-made man than is a member of any other profession. You can outsell the born salesman if you know what to do and when and how to do it. You must practice effective techniques until they become an ingrained part of your personality and manner of selling. After a brief trial you may feel that a certain sales technique is ineffective, but it may turn out to be extremely productive if you develop it to the point where prospects no longer see it for what it is. You know, of course, that for the most effective selling, you should not reveal that any special technique is being used. It has often been said that a sales manager can develop mediocre salesmen, but the outstanding, star-level salesman must develop himself. Attitude and viewpoints you can control. It has been proved again and again that attitude is more important to sales success than aptitude.

Be Proud You're a Salesman

Before you get into the work of improving your sales techniques, take a moment to set up a perspective or frame of reference. You will agree that all business starts with orders. No orders, no sales revenue. No sales revenue, no business. This simple fact makes the salesman the prime mover of our economy. By making a sale that is formalized into an order, the salesman starts the chain reaction that turns the wheels of our profit-oriented economy. The customer's freedom of choice is the factor which makes the salesman the keystone of our economic life. Freedom of decision in the market place is the first and greatest of freedoms. Should we ever lose that, our marketing system and our other freedoms will wither away.

Al N. Sears, retired vice-president of Remington-Rand Division of the Sperry Rand Corporation, expresses it this way:

"What is a sale? It is an expression of a value judgment, arrived at in the mind of a man or woman who has the ability to buy—and the capacity to pay. That is a very simple observation, but it will bear examination—because it is fundamental to the subject of Marketing Intelligence. Let me remind you that the subject matter of economics is not such things as prices, demand, supply, or the organization of production. They are the results of overt actions. The subject matter of economics, of which marketing is an important part, is the value judgments of many millions of men and women.

"What are these value judgments that control marketing? They are results of a comparison made in the human mind. The comparison can be put this way: I see or feel a need or experience a dissatisfaction. Call that Condition A. I am offered a product or service that can meet that need or remove that dissatisfaction, at a given price. Call that Condition B. I compare Condition A to Condition B. If A is more intense than B, I buy. If B is more intense than A, I keep my money. Since I, like everybody else, can conjure more wants and needs than I have money—I must choose among them and satisfy only those my means permit, foregoing the others.

"The job of the salesman is to educate me to perceive—or to motivate me to feel that I will be better off by buying than by not buying. It is the job of the rest of the people who are the marketing system to make the price I must pay to meet a need—or remove a dissatisfaction—the lowest it can be. If you will keep this simple model in mind when you think about selling, you can focus your attention on the essential facts you need and avoid a lot of extraneous matters.

"Since sales are made in the minds of buyers, for they can be made nowhere else, we can regard the sales process as:

> Telling the right story
> To the right people
> At the right time
> In the right way."*

* Taken from text of a lecture sponsored by the Department of Industrial Administration of Yale University and the National Association of Manufacturers, April 27, 1958, pp. 1–2.

However, even though the sales process is essentially the same in any type of selling, the application of the process is quite different in different types of selling. Selling to dealers is quite different from selling to industrial buyers or ultimate consumers. Selling power shovels is different from selling aspirin or life insurance. Therefore, it is important to your sales success for you to select the type of selling that you are most interested in and for which you are best fitted.

Specialized Selling

This is an age of specialization in selling.* No longer can a man assert, "I am going out and sell," and feel that his success is assured because he has mastered a few basic techniques. Sales techniques today must be adapted to specific products or services, different sorts of buyers, and various types of situations. However, making such adaptations requires time and practice. Skill in meeting specific situations in selling makes the difference between the born salesman of yesterday and the professional salesman of today.

The modern salesman's job was aptly described by J. Donald Staunton, director of training of National Starch Products, Inc., in this way:

"What does the salesman do?

"He brings personality, organizational skills, product knowledge, and market knowledge to bear on the problems of moving goods. He works for several people: his customers, his firm, and himself. Today, as industry becomes more complex, the demands on the salesman are greater and he needs to have more technical knowledge, more control over his own personality, and more organizational and selling skill to do his job."†

Now you may ask, "Where and how can I start to improve?"

Outline of a Sale

One of the quickest and easiest ways of improving yourself is to impress firmly upon your memory this three-step outline of a sale.

* See Charles L. Lapp, *Successful Selling Strategies,* New York: McGraw-Hill, 1957, pp. 317–343. A discussion of how to find the right sales job for you, written by Charles R. Frederick of the National Retail Farm Equipment Association.

† J. Donald Staunton, "I Didn't Raise My Boy to be a Salesman," *Management Review,* March, 1958, pp. 9–13.

When you sell you're trying to:

1. Bring the prospect from freezing to boiling.
2. Recognize when the prospect is at the boiling point.
3. Persuade him to sign the order (that is, close him), after you've brought him up to the boiling point.

Sell while you tell to bring prospects from freezing to boiling. You can sell while you tell if you get commitments from prospects.

To obtain an order from a prospect, you must be able to recognize when he is at the boiling (i.e., decision-making) point. He is at that point when you've obtained enough commitments from him. You obtain commitments by asking the prospect questions to which he's likely to agree. This subject is discussed at length in Chapter 4.

The proper steps to induce the prospect to sign the order (that is, to close him) after you've brought him up to boiling are covered fully in future chapters. However, after you've obtained a sufficient number of commitments (usually a minimum of three), it is surprising how little urging is necessary to get the prospect to say Yes or to put his name on the dotted line. But remember that you must *ask* the prospect to say Yes. Even though he wants to, he may never tell you if you don't ask him. The more orders you get, the more money you make, and the greater your contribution to our standard of living.

Assistance This Book Can Give You

So much for the over-all concept of selling. The remainder of this book deals with specific suggestions. Primary consideration is given to field-tested techniques. You will find ideas on how to add a positive touch to your effort. A step-by-step method for developing your sales story is discussed. You will see how a planned sales story can be adapted to specific prospects, products, and sales situations. Questions that can be used to gain acceptance of prospects to your sales proposition are recommended. A variety of ways to ask for an order are illustrated.

Such expert touches for more effective selling as overcoming objections, handling the price shopper, and outselling competition are discussed for the benefit of those who have mastered the fundamentals of selling. Practical techniques are suggested for handling recurring as well as unusual selling situations.

The final chapters show how you as a salesman can increase your earnings by finding more and better prospects, by making profitable return calls, and by giving your customers more effective service. Suggested techniques are illustrated by actual sales interviews, which can be adapted to your products or service and to your customers.

And lastly, there are check lists and thought-provokers for your convenience in reviewing fudamentals and specifics. No one is born with a mastery of selling. Your mastery of selling depends on you. Get started now to improve your sales batting average.

SUMMARY THOUGHT-PROVOKERS

Give attention to those appearance factors over which you have control.

Develop your own personal characteristics. (No one is born with social graces.)

Remember your objective—to get the order.

Use this book to assist you to self-improve.

KEY REVIEW POINTS FOR
SELF-IMPROVEMENT

What can you do to improve your appearance? Ask your wife or a close friend—or your mirror.

What aspects of your personality are most, or least, pleasing to others? Ask yourself—and be honest.

After each no-sale interview, ask yourself if you moved the prospect in the direction of closing (the boiling point). If so, how did you? And if not, why didn't you?

To sell more, **develop** your personality
To **improve** your selling techniques, know
the **what** and **why** of selling

Chapter 2

Selling with a Positive Touch

Confidence in yourself
Approaching the prospect
Knowing what to say
Asking for the order

As you have seen, many salesmen work by impulse, by intuition, by instinct. They do the right thing some of the time but they do not have a plan they can follow to get good results consistently. Their conceptions of their methods are usually both vague and erroneous. They have little, if any, understanding of the science of salesmanship.

Feel You Can Sell and You Will Sell

If you have a proper viewpoint toward selling, you've already a better opportunity for success than many of your fellow salesmen. By the time you've absorbed the ideas in the remainder of this book you'll know much more about selling than most of the men competing with you. Each day, as you study, you will find it easier to outsell competitive salesmen. But never forget that the proper attitude toward selling and toward your customers is as important to your success as is skill with words. Your point of view is silently, if not audibly, projected to your prospects.

Finding and Meeting New Prospects

Acquire the ability to find prospects. This is discussed in detail in Chapter 12. While some expert salesmen spend a reasonable amount of time and effort on prospecting, there are many who consider this wasteful. They ask, "Why spend the time of a high-priced salesman doing the work that lower-cost canvassers or advertising can handle?"

Of course, if the management of your company is able to provide you continuously with all the prospects you need to keep you productive, you aren't going to throw these gifts into the wastebasket. Remember, however, that some day the present stream of prospects may dwindle to a trickle. Or you may change your affiliation to a company and a product where you constantly need to add to your supply of prospects by your own efforts.

A very important skill to develop is that of approaching a strange person. If you approach him with confidence and consideration, ninety-nine times out of a hundred you'll be greeted and treated with the same politeness and consideration that you yourself show. If you're rude and gruff and tough to the prospect, the prospect will mirror your attitude and be rude and gruff and tough to you. *You're* going to be pleasant and polite, aren't you? So the prospect will treat *you* pleasantly and politely. Most people will tend to treat you as you treat them.

You will have to do one more thing, however, to ensure a pleasant reception. *You must put yourself in the prospect's place* and make certain that you aren't barging in on him at an inconvenient time, when even a minute will be begrudged to you. Putting yourself in the prospect's place is referred to by the psychologists as "empathy." Dr. Donald A. Laird and Eleanor C. Laird, in their valuable book *Practical Business Psychology,* define empathy as "an impersonal recognition of what lies behind another person's thoughts and actions." Empathy is different from sympathy, which is based upon imagining how others feel. People do not, however, always feel as you imagine they do. Empathy, in contrast to sympathy, is rational rather than emotional. Empathy makes it possible for you to recognize the true nature of another's behavior.

AN EXAMPLE OF AN EFFECTIVE APPROACH

If you'll incorporate the following introduction into your approach and use it essentially *word for word,* adapting it to your product, line, or prospects IN EVERY INSTANCE where you don't have a previously made appointment, you'll insure a pleasant, prompt reception for yourself. This is it:

"Mr. Kane, I'm not here to talk to you *now*. When can you spare *two minutes* to answer a question?"

Notice that you don't *try* to make your sale then and there. Instead, you ask for an appointment for a later interview. To understand the attitude of the prospect on whom you call without previous appointment, put yourself in his place. The businessman has many problems to occupy his attention without talking to you. The same is true of the housewife. You may be approaching either of them at the moment most inconvenient for them.

In both cases you'll find that your statement, "I'm not here to talk to you *now;* when can you spare two minutes to answer a question?" will be most disarming. The great majority of answers will be, "I guess I can spare two minutes right now. What is the question?"

Your reply to this is, "Would this afternoon or tomorrow be a better time for you to take a few minutes to see the newest development in transistors?" Or, "Would this afternoon or tomorrow be a better time for me to take a few minutes and make some measurements, and give you a free estimate on an automatic heating installation that will give you and your family a more comfortable and healthier home, and that will save you money?"

Notice that you try for a definite appointment by mentioning a specific day. If the date is set for tomorrow, be sure to confirm the time too, by suggesting a definite hour to the prospect. Do *not* ask, *"When* can I take a few minutes and make some measurements . . . ?"

Now and then, in answer to your opening question, someone will reply, "I'm too busy to spare even one second, now or in the future." If you get that answer, unless the individual concerned is a very special, super-deluxe, two-hundred-carat prospect, say, "Thank you, good-by!" and leave. Neither you nor he will have any hard words, and there are many, many more prospects, better than this one, who may be more receptive to your efforts.

The essential fact to remember is that the proper approach by you, in the proper manner, will assure you a pleasant reception. Try the one given above—not once, but dozens and dozens of times. After you've used it two or three hundred times and it's working for you, perhaps you can think of a better one.

Should the brusque prospect be someone whom you simply *must* see, you'll have to try again, possibly several times. You may have to use different approaches—introductions from mutual friends, letters, telegrams, telephone calls, or something creatively unusual—to pave the way for you to get an appointment with him.

Knowing What to Say

You should never find yourself thinking as too many salesmen do, "I don't know what to say," or saying, "I'm a new man in this business and I haven't learned that yet."

If you do, this will shake the confidence of the prospect in you and also lower his esteem for your company. He'll feel that your management shouldn't have sent a beginner to call on a man of his importance and waste his time. You will have lost the respect of the prospect. His pride may be hurt, and he may even be deeply insulted at such treatment to an individual of his standing.

The reason you react in this way is that you haven't familiarized yourself with your prospect, your product or service, or a planned sales story. After all, if you had to call on one hundred of the most important people in the world and say to each of them, "One, two, three, four, five," you wouldn't be afraid to do that, would you, because you know how to count and you're confident that this knowledge won't escape you.

THREE STEPS TO MAKE CERTAIN YOU
HAVE SOMETHING TO SAY

To avoid being put into the embarrassing situation of not having an answer, follow these three steps:

The first step: Study your product and your sales story until you know both thoroughly. Since your study may take considerable time—delaying you painfully in getting out into the field—you can take this step in two stages.

Stage one: Someone has said that an educated man is not one who *knows* everything but one who *knows where to find* everything. To educate yourself rapidly, go through your sales portfolios and your technical manuals again and again, not

24

trying to memorize the facts and figures they contain but *to remember where they are*. If necessary, place slips of paper, appropriately marked, at pages that you feel may require frequent reference. Then, if a prospect asks for information, you can answer, "I'll let you see what our engineering department says about that." And you flip the book open to the place.

Stage two: Next make frequent reference to the facts and figures you've pinpointed, as set forth above. The oftener you look at them, the sooner they'll be impressed upon your memory. Thus, if you're active in the field, you'll find that you quickly learn the technical data and other facts about the product that were presented in your factory or district office training. It won't be too long until you've mastered the essential information.

The second step: Put it on paper to help you remember it. Write or type on a card or sheet of paper a legible, concise outline containing the key words of your sales story. Put this in front of you before you begin your presentation. You'll probably not need to refer to it, but it will be there to reassure you and refresh your memory; it will prompt you in case of necessity. You can use it openly. Just tell the prospect, "Mr. Lewis, I'm putting this outline here and may refer to it from time to time. We have so many outstanding selling points that I want to make absolutely sure that you don't miss even one. You won't mind my handling it this way, will you?"

After you have given your sales presentation a number of times you will find you won't need the outline before you. However, you may find this technique so effective that you continue to use it.

The third step: Equip yourself with some intelligent phrases for use when, in spite of your preparation, you really don't know the answer. For instance, since no one is expected to know everything, you won't lose face by saying, "I don't know, but I'll find out."

Usually, it's better to make no comment other than your intention to find out the answer for him. However, if the occasion requires you to elaborate on this reply, something along the lines of the following carries little risk: "I'm glad you asked that question, Mr. Means, for in all my experience you're the first person who's asked it of me, and you've made me want to know the answer too. I'll be in touch with the factory today and can probably give you the information by telephone —I'll call them right now, if you want me to. Otherwise you will get a letter from me with the answer in the next few days. . . . Many thanks. . . . Say, do you have any other questions?"

Ask for the Order—Be More Than a Conversationalist

The culmination of your sales effort, of course, comes when you get the order. But some salesmen hesitate to try for the close because they don't know when or how to make the attempt. It is easy to recognize the right time to close by the number of commitments you've received. If you've been actively developing your sales demonstration and have tried for at least three commitments, you may have the prospect sufficiently convinced to justify trying for a close.

When you try for the order, the prospect will say either Yes or No. If he says No, he isn't also going to take you out and shoot you at sunrise, is he? Nor will he put you into the torture chamber with poisonous snakes.

That word No is not necessarily a total rejection of your proposition. *First,* it is a clue as to how well you're progressing and where you need to strengthen your presentation. *Second,* there is a way to use that word No as a springboard to getting the order. This is covered in Chapter 6.

KEY REVIEW POINTS FOR SELF-IMPROVEMENT

In what ways can you show prospects that you wish to treat them pleasantly and politely?

What questions will disarm a prospect whom you want to see but with whom you have no appointment?

How can you be sure you know what to say?

How can you know the right time to try for the close?

Have **confidence in yourself** and others will have confidence in you

Chapter 3

Developing a Sales Story

How you can use a **planned** story
Principles of **constructing** a story
How to **develop** your own story to **sell**
   while you **tell**

ONE OF the surest methods of producing sales is the use of a planned sales story. Too many salesmen present their information in a way which has come about by accident. Certain things work with Mr. A and Mr. B, so these things are incorporated into the presentation. Soon the story is crystallized through constant use. The only trouble is that the presentation is not effective with prospects D, E, and X, Y, Z. A *planned* sales story, on the other hand, is a blueprint which has proved effective and can easily be adjusted to each selling situation.

Everyone Should Use a Planned Sales Story

There are three groups of salesmen who may be inclined to underestimate the importance of the planned sales story.

SELLING STAPLE MERCHANDISE

The first group consists of those who sell staple merchandise to the same customers year in and year out. Repeat orders give these salesmen their income.

These men can profit by having a planned sales story at their fingertips. Naturally, they aren't going to give it to the same buyer in the same company each of the three or four times a year they see him. Buyers do change, however. "Mr. Edwards is no longer with the company," the receptionist informs you. "Mr. Foster is now head of that department. Do you want to see *him?*"

Of course you do. And a planned sales story will help you with the new buyer.

Even if Mr. Edwards is still the buyer and no change is contemplated, a reminder to him of some of the points of superiority of your company, your product, and your service may well be in order. After all, haven't some competitors been to see Mr. Edwards during your absence, claiming that their company, their product, and their service are superior to yours? Are you going to make it easy for them to supersede you and eventually take over this account? On each call, some reminders and some commitments from your planned sales story, covering your company, your merchandise, and your service, can be useful in keeping your customer on your team. Again, the salesman of staple merchandise will find a planned sales story extremely helpful when calling upon prospects who do not now handle his brand but whom he would like to convert into customers.

SELLING DIFFERENT TYPES OF PROSPECTS

The second group of salesmen who may rebel against the use of a planned sales story are those who say, "All prospects aren't alike. Each human being is different. You can't tell the same story in the same way to each man. To be successful, you've got to adapt your sales presentation to fit both the needs and the individuality of the person to whom you're talking."

Everything these salesmen say is correct. Prospects aren't the same. Each human being is different. There are plenty of people for whom you'll have to shift the emphasis from one point to another when you tell your planned sales story. And certainly you should adapt your sales presentation to fit both the needs and the individuality of the person to whom you're talking. But this is not an argument against the proper use of a sales story. A planned sales story must be adjusted to different prospects. However, a planned sales story gives you the basic points from which to draw upon and adapt. A planned sales story is not a one-way conversation. Planned participation from your prospect should be built into your crystallized sales story.

SELLING DIFFERENT TYPES OF MERCHANDISE

The third group of salesmen who may protest against the

use of a planned sales story comprises those who sell more than one type of merchandise or whose product has more than one end use. The answer is that a planned sales story should be developed for each product or service and for each end use of your product or service.

An example of the latter is the life-insurance salesman. He says, "Fundamentally, I sell only one product—life insurance. Yet my prospects vary in the end use they're going to make of the proceeds of the policy I'm offering them. You wouldn't expect me to tell the same story to four prospects with different insurance objectives, would you? Take, for example, as one prospect, the childless couple who want to provide retirement income for their old age; or the man who purchases a policy to assure a college education for his son; or the partners or members of a closed corporation who want protection and continuity for their business should one of the group die; or the managers who are setting up and administering a pension fund for their employees." There are many other examples, but these four should be enough to illustrate this point.

When a salesman is selling several different types of merchandise or a product with many end uses, he will construct a planned sales story for each different type of merchandise or for each of the several end uses for his product or service. But he will find that he can use a fair share of word-for-word duplication in the various stories. Each planned sales presentation undoubtedly would contain persuasive references to the features of his products or services and to the reliability of his company. Each would also stress the good service given customers, not only in prompt attention to orders, but also in giving advice and other assistance.

Basic Organization of a Planned Sales Story

The basis of your planned sales story is contained in the following plan:

Step 1. Three reasons why the prospect should buy the type of product (or service) you are selling.*

---

* You may ask why three reasons instead of one, five, or nine. Through their experience in selling and teaching, the authors have found the typical individual can remember three easily. Less than three points may be sufficient with some prospects; however, it always pays to have some selling points in reserve should they be needed.

Step 2. Three reasons why the prospect should buy your product or service instead of any competing brand in the same field.

Step 3. Three reasons why the prospect should buy your product now.

Your story in that form will probably be interesting, but it will still lack effectiveness. Remember, you're trying to bring the prospect from freezing up to boiling. You recall that to do this you not only must develop a good story but also must obtain commitments. You'll note that committing questions in sets of three are indicated below for major points or features.

While planning your sales story in advance, then, prepare an outline similar to the one below:

Step 1. Three reasons why the prospect needs the *type* of product or service you are selling:

    a. Statement and explanation of first reason
        1. Committing question
        2. Committing question
        3. Committing question
    b. Statement and explanation of second reason
        1. Committing question
        2. Committing question
        3. Committing question
    c. Statement and explanation of third reason
        1. Committing question
        2. Committing question
        3. Committing question

Step 2. Three features or reasons why the prospect should buy *your* product or service instead of any competing brand in the same field:

    a. Explanation and demonstration of first feature
        1. Committing question
        2. Committing question
        3. Committing question
    b. Explanation and demonstration of second feature
        1. Committing question
        2. Committing question
        3. Committing question

   c. Explanation and demonstration of third feature
      1. Committing question
      2. Committing question
      3. Committing question

Step 3. Three reasons why the prospect should buy your product or service *now:*

   a. Statement and explanation of first reason
      1. Committing question
      2. Committing question
      3. Committing question
   b. Statement and explanation of second reason
      1. Committing question
      2. Committing question
      3. Committing question
   c. Statement and explanation of third reason
      1. Committing question
      2. Committing question
      3. Committing question

It will pay you to stick to the above outline as closely as is practicable when preparing your sales story in advance. You can impress this outline upon your memory by calling it the "1-2-3 Formula." You'll like the results you get from its use.

CONSTRUCTING THE OUTLINE OF A SALES STORY: A PRACTICAL EXAMPLE

Let's consider automobiles. All makes are essentially similar. Accessories that were once unique, such as power steering and automatic clutchless transmission, are now provided by all makes at comparable price levels. The sales story therefore becomes longer and perhaps more complicated. It's impossible to foresee which of the developments embodied in the automobiles of today will appeal to a specific prospect. At least one order has been closed because a salesman demonstrated the rear-seat folding arm rest, while a competitive salesman whose car also had this item neglected to mention it in his sales story.

To construct a planned sales story for an automobile, follow the three steps outlined on page 29.

Step 1. List all the reasons why the prospect should buy the type of product or service you are selling. When you have completed the first step of the proposed automobile sales story, you should come up with not three, but six possible buying motives:

1. Financial advantage
2. Comfort
3. Safety
4. Prestige
5. Convenience
6. Health

You can use three of the above and still have three as a reserve.

Step 2. First, write three major reasons why the prospect should buy *your* product or service rather than any competing brand in the same field. Then, list all desirable features of the car you are selling, as fast as they occur to you. Your list should include some of these:

Power-flow automatic drive
Power steering
Power brakes (optional)
V-8 engine
Riding and driving comfort
Rugged body construction
Advanced design
Operating economy
Dependability, reliability, and long experience of manufacturer and dealer
Vibrationless balanced engine
Easily adjustable front seat
Convenient parking brake and warning light
Quiet body mountings
Tinted glareless safety glass
Directional turn signal with automatic cutoff

Wide seats
Comfort-zone heating
Draftless ventilation
Wide-vision windshield
Trouble-free air conditioning
Automatically tuning radio
Windshield washer
Automatic back-up lights
No-glare rear-vision mirror
Accelerator starting
Dual-action ignition switch
Easily read instrument panel with adjustable lighting
Individual 4-wheel coil springs
X-girder steel frame
Reverse-action shock absorbers
Luxury body
Tubeless tires
Extra-large brake bands

Now rearrange your list in more logical order, placing each feature under the reason (you wrote down three) to which it most closely pertains. Your list should be similar to the following:

1. Advanced design

Luxury body	Easily read instrument panel
Rugged body construction	Dual-action ignition switch
Quiet body mountings	Convenient parking brake and
Tubeless tires	warning light
Extra-large brake bands	Wide-vision windshield
Easily adjustable front seat	Windshield washer
Accelerator starting	Operating economy

2. Riding and driving comfort and ease of handling

Power-flow automatic drive	Power brakes (optional)
X-girder steel frame	Wide seats
Individual four-wheel coil springs	No-glare rear-vision mirror
	Draftless ventilation
Reverse-action shock absorbers	Comfort-zone heating
V-8 engine	Direction turn signal with auto-
Vibrationless balanced engine	matic cutoff
Power steering	Tinted glareless safety glass

3. Dependability, reliability, and long experience of dealer and manufacturer.

Step 3. Write down all the reasons you can think of why the prospect should buy an automobile now, such as:

1. Financial advantage
2. Dependability (contingent upon the condition of prospect's present car)
3. Safety (contingent upon condition of prospect's car)
4. Comfort
5. Pride of ownership
6. Health (power steering reduces heart strain)

Developing a Planned Sales Story for Your Own Product or Service

You are now ready to start the construction of your own planned sales story, in the form of a sales-presentation dialogue.

First you make an outline for your own product or service following the "1-2-3 Formula." Remember that most products or services have exclusive and unique features. Incorporating at least three of these into your basic outline will give you a powerful, hard-hitting sales story that is not excessively long or difficult to learn.

After you complete the outline, write out a complete story, word for word, phrase for phrase, and sentence for sentence as you feel it might develop. Naturally, you will never *use* your story word for word, phrase for phrase, or sentence for sentence as you have written it—and there's no reason why you should. On the other hand, a complete story will give you something to draw upon and to modify for each sales situation, which will help you to lead your prospects to a buying decision.

In writing and in actually following your planned sales story, remember that when it can be obtained without protest, it's most helpful to obtain the name and address of another prospect. (This is usually easier to obtain at the beginning of the interview than at the end.)

As you write out your own dialogue, if you should find the constant repetition of committing questions monotonous and even annoyingly "choppy" in your planned sales presentations, keep in mind that, in actual sales, prospects are probably talking even more than is portrayed in your written example. Moreover, in the field, there are pauses and interruptions, and sometimes even intentional delays, between the various features as the salesman moves through a carefully planned sales presentation.

Pauses, interruptions, or a smile tend to make the actual use of a planned sales presentation much smoother than it appears to be in the written version. Moreover, the monotonous effect of the multiple committing questions will be lessened in many cases, where it may be unnecessary to go through the *entire* planned sales presentation before closing the sale.

A GOOD SALES STORY IS MORE THAN TALKING

"Developing" a good story is slightly different from "telling" a good story. When you develop your story, you add to the telling of it:

1. Prospect participation.
2. Demonstration sales helps, models, or actual samples.

INCORPORATE BASIC BUYING MOTIVES INTO YOUR SALES STORY

Each prospect has many points of similarity with every other prospect. For all are members of the human race, and certain similar motives activate almost every human being. Your sales story will be most effective if it incorporates and dramatizes some of these universal motives and if it stresses those that appeal most strongly to the individual prospect on whom you're calling. Adjustment of your planned sales story to fit each individual is *reaction selling*.

Let's consider some of these universal motives or appeals:

Health—Every normal person wants to protect and/or improve the health of himself and his loved ones.

Financial advantages—Can you think of anyone who isn't interested in either making more money, or in saving money by reducing expenses, or in providing for the financial well-being of himself and his family?

Comfort—Is there anyone who wants to be uncomfortable? If your product adds to comfort, it has universal appeal.

Convenience—Everybody wants to be relieved of drudgery. People don't mind working, but they don't want to waste their efforts or to do work that isn't necessary. What homeowner who has installed automatic oil or gas heating, for example, would choose to go back to the drudgery of furnace-tending?

Cleanliness—Even animals attempt to keep their nests and burrows clean. Few human beings live in dirty homes or care to work in slovenly offices or plants, if a product is available within their means to correct this condition.

Increased property valuation—When people own homes or factories or other buildings or structures or equipment, they want to maintain the value of their possessions. They want to protect their investment and to increase its value, if possible, by keeping their property modern and in good condition.

Usable space—If you have a product such as a roof insulation that will "make an attic into a third floor," or such as automatic oil or gas heating that will allow you to "make your basement into a recreation room," it will have widespread appeal.

Increase in the happiness, well-being, and efficiency of a family or employees—This motive might also be included under the "Financial advantages" heading. For instance, employers know that a product or service that improves the happiness, well-being, or efficiency of their employees pays off in cold cash.

The foregoing are a few examples of motives or appeals that

have universal influence. You can think of others. Some of the above will apply to the product or service you're selling. Those that do should be incorporated into your planned sales story.

BE READY TO ADAPT TO SPECIFIC PROSPECTS

On actual sales, of course, you should adapt the outline to suit the particular individual and the existing situation. For example, in an air-conditioning sales interview situation, if the prospect greets you with, "I'm going to purchase air-conditioning equipment; tell me about your unit," you wouldn't go through Step 1 of the outline, "Three reasons why the prospect needs the *type* of product or service you are selling." Even in such a situation, however, it usually helps to make a sale to ask the prospect, "Do you mind telling me why you're going to install air conditioning? Your answer will assist me in determining how well our equipment will fit your needs."

When, as, and if the prospect gives his reasons for buying, he's beginning to move himself upward from 32°. His repetition of his reasons strengthens his desire to make the purchase.

Again, unless the prospect is particularly resistant, or unless you've been weak in presenting Step 2—"Three reasons why the prospect should buy *your* product or service instead of any competing brand in the same field"—it may be that in many cases you can secure the order without presenting Step 3— "Three reasons why the prospect should buy your product or service *now*."

Suppose, for example, the prospect has told you why he is interested in purchasing air-conditioning equipment before you begin your sales presentation. Suppose, moreover, you explain and demonstrate two of the exclusive features of your brand. And suppose that you've asked for, and obtained, three commitments for each of these features. That gives you a total of six commitments (without including in this count the prospect's description of his reasons for being interested in air conditioning). These six commitments may mean that the prospect is ready to sign the order.

A planned sales story will be stronger and harder hitting, because it is logically planned and because commitments are consciously and intentionally included at strategic points. The real payoff comes, however, in making adaptations for specific customers.

SUMMARY THOUGHT-PROVOKERS

A summary of this chapter on developing a sales story may be helpful.

To sell while you tell—that is, to bring the prospect from as low as freezing up to boiling—you're advised to:

Develop a good sales story.

Provide for prospect participation.

Adjust your sales story to each prospect and sales situation.

KEY REVIEW POINTS FOR
SELF-IMPROVEMENT

What three things are you trying to do when you sell?

To what plan should your planned sales story adhere?

Write down as many reasons as you can think of why anyone should buy *your* type of product or service. Choose the three strongest reasons from this list.

Write down as many reasons as you can think of why anyone should buy your product or service *now*. Choose the three strongest reasons from this list.

Do you see that, except for the appropriate committing questions, you have gathered together the basic outline for your planned sales presentation?

What is the difference between developing and telling a sales story?

Improve your sales story to improve your
reception and the **reaction** of prospects

Chapter 4

Using Committing Questions

Determine **why** prospects **don't buy**
Improve through **questions**
Don't **convince;** let them **judge**
How to get commitments from a prospect
Commitments that **lead** to a **sale**

AFTER READING this far you may be inclined to ask: "Don't the authors know that selling any product or service isn't merely describing its features and getting commitments and giving a demonstration and presenting a planned sales story? They're ignoring the most important problem of all—that is, how to get the prospect to give you the sought-for commitments."

Determine Why Prospects Don't Buy

If a prospect says, "I am not buying now," ask, "Well, then, do you mind telling me what is holding up your decision?"

Should he say, "I still don't like that compressor on your equipment," you can answer, "I understand that is one feature you have some question about. But don't the other six features you do like overbalance it, particularly as we've never had a service call on our compressors?"

If he replies, "No, they don't!" then say something like this: "Will you talk to two or three people who own our equipment and who've actually lived with it? Thus you can see for yourself, and hear from actual owners, how much or how little trouble this feature that worries you has caused them."

If he won't go with you, arrange to secure several testimonial letters from your local users, and make an appointment to take them to him.

Use Questions to Improve Your Selling Effectiveness

Consciously and deliberately try for commitments throughout your sales presentation. As we said before, if you ask a question and obtain an answer, you're getting a commitment. The prospect has put himself on record.

Sometimes the prospect gives commitments by agreement without your asking an outright question. Suppose you say, "More and more railroads are becoming completely dieselized," and he replies, "That's true," he's given you a commitment by agreement. Most commitments from prospects, however, will come, and should come, from planned questions, deliberately inserted by you at proper intervals in your sales presentation. A declaratory statement is a means of direct suggestion to a prospect, whereas a question is a means of indirect suggestion. As Pierre Martineau points out, "Indirect suggestion avoids clashing with the other individual's system of beliefs, which is his self."[*]

A good sales presentation should be well seasoned with questions. Yet, like food, it should not be overseasoned. Three types of questions may be used for effective selling: those to secure interest and attention, those you ask when you secure the prospect's participation in a sales presentation, and those you use to close a sale.

PREPARE YOUR QUESTIONS IN ADVANCE

The committing questions you prepare in advance should follow the outline of your planned sales story, discussed in Chapter 3. Therefore it might be well to take another look at a planned sales story, this time for making the sale of a room air conditioner. The outline for this sales story might be as follows:

1. Three reasons for buying air conditioning
   a. Comfort: better rest, no sweltering
   b. Health: better sleeping
   c. Financial:
      1. Save money: fewer doctors' bills
      2. Make money: by doing better work on the job because of better physical condition

* Pierre Martineau, *Motivation in Advertising*, New York: McGraw-Hill, 1957, p. 129.

2. Why to buy our brand rather than any other
   a. Strong manufacturer
   b. Dependable local distributor
   c. Good engineering: one moving part, self-oiling, permanently sealed, each part made for the others, assembled in own factory, nontoxic refrigerant
3. Why to buy *now*
   a. To be ready to use during the first hot or humid weather
   b. To get an unhurried installation
   c. Payments begin at the same time as if you buy later

Now all that is needed, after each sales point is developed for each of the above points, is to develop committing questions to find out if each sales point is accepted by the prospect.

QUESTIONS CAN BE STRONGER THAN STATEMENTS

Questions can often take the place of declaratory statements most effectively. In fact, the stronger the statement, the more desirable it is that you should phrase it in the form of a question. (The reason for this is that you can try for a hard-hitting commitment rather than a weak one.)

For example, suppose your product is manufactured by a billion-dollar company that has been in business for fifty years. If you made a statement to that effect it would run something like this: "Mrs. Long, our dishwasher is manufactured by a billion-dollar company, in business for fifty years. If you invest in our dishwasher, there's very little likelihood that in case you ever need a part you'd be owning an orphan."

Changing these two statements to questions, they might sound as follows: "Mrs. Long, don't you think it would give you added confidence and protection to purchase a dishwasher manufactured by a billion-dollar company such as ours, in business fifty years? . . . If you invest in our dishwasher there'd be little chance that, should you ever need a part, you'd own an orphan, would there?"

EXAMPLES OF TYPICAL COMMITTING QUESTIONS:

There's nothing difficult or mysterious about these committing questions. They're just ordinary conversation that any man can use and any man can understand.

"That's strong and sturdy and well made, isn't it?"

"Do you notice how comfortable that seat is?"

"All people like to save money, don't they?"

"It'll be a relief to get rid of those repair bills, won't it?"

"That's good engineering isn't it?"

"That'll look good in your living room, won't it?"

"Have I made it clear how that saves you money?"

"It's a big comfort to have pickup like that when you need it, isn't it?"

"Nice big closets, aren't they?"

You've probably noticed that many of these are simply a statement of the selling point, with an "isn't it?" or "aren't they?" added at the end to get the commitment.

Remember, if you want to increase your sales productivity, try changing strong statements in your sales presentation to committing questions, as above.

There are countless committing words. It will pay you to find them and file them in your memory, and to use as many as possible, such as:

"Mr. Mason, do you *understand* how this feature saves you money?"

"Mr. Mason, wouldn't you *like* not to be bothered with the work? This installation will do it for you and Mrs. Mason. Wouldn't that be a relief?"

"Mr. Parker, don't you *feel* you and your company will benefit if you protect the health and safety of your working force?"

"Mr. Neeley, do you *appreciate* the freedom from service that the sealed-in, self-oiling Rotomaster unit provides?"

Don't Convince the Prospect— Let Him Be the Judge

Be careful of the word "convince"! Many salesmen use it in a dangerous way. They say something like the following to the prospect: "I'm sure that I can *convince* you that our product is the one you should have."

Don't make the mistake of telling this to the prospect. As soon as you do, he's apt to put up his guard and to say to himself, "This chap thinks he can convince me, does he? Well, I'll show him! I'm no weakling. I know my own mind, and nobody can make it up for me."

Should the prospect say of one of your features or specifications, "Mr. Johnson, that's all very interesting, but you haven't *convinced* me that your power steering is better than your competitor's," a good reply is along these lines:

"Please give me a minute, Mr. Ogden. Evidently I haven't told you enough about the features of our automobile. Let me answer both sides of this question before you make up your mind. There are certain phases of this problem that will help you make up your mind in your own way. Then *you* be the judge."

Use Commitments to Test the Buying Temperature of All Your Prospects

Not only do commitments put the prospect on record and assist in selling him. They also give you a quick and frequent means of testing your own progress. For example, if you try for a commitment and the prospect gives you an answer different from the one you seek, you know that here's a point you haven't made clear to him. You must use further effort to get him on your side. You may have to repeat or develop your demonstration of the point in question and explain it to him more fully to secure his agreement.

Sometimes his disagreement with you on a given feature cannot be resolved, no matter how skillful your efforts. In such a case you'll find it effective not to make an issue of it. A statement such as the following may bypass the dangerous point smoothly: "That's an interesting subject, Mr. Idell. As I've indicated, our engineering department has done a great deal of research in regard to that point. Actually, we've not had a single service call. We have some other features, too, that I know you'll want to consider"—and go on from there to present other unique advantages of your product. (Note that the word "point" is used rather than a word with negative suggestion, such as "objection.")

The committing technique might be summarized in the following way:

1. Agree with the prospect's reasoning.
2. Show that your company had a similar problem when it took on its present line (or when it designed the line, if you represent the manufacturer).

3. State the sales points of your equipment that persuaded your company to choose it rather than other makes or types.

USUALLY THERE IS NO SHORT CUT TO A SALE

You'll recall that usually three or more commitments from the prospect are necessary to make a sale. Of course, if he gives you only one commitment and says, "All right, I'll sign the order," or, "What do I do to make the purchase?" you don't need to try for more.

Some salesmen will receive one commitment from the prospect and immediately attempt to close. For example, the salesman asks, "Do you have confidence in the Harkness Corporation, whom I represent?" The prospect replies, "I certainly do! You have a splendid company." Then the salesman, stimulated by this commitment, attempts to close without giving the demonstration of his product and its sales features. Consciously or unconsciously, this is an attempt at a short cut that too often fails.

If you liken yourself to a fisherman trying to catch a large, heavy fish with only a light line and a small, weak hook, you'll see the importance of obtaining several commitments. The prospect, of course, takes the place of the large, heavy fish. (This analogy intends no disrespect to the prospect!) A commitment is like the light line with the weak hook. You couldn't land a big fish with only one fragile hook or with a weak line, could you? But you could if you used enough small hooks on small lines, couldn't you?

STRONG VS. WEAK SELLING

When you're selling an idea, such as trying for a raise or applying for a position, it is of course essential that you both tell a good story and get commitments. Point out your achievements. *To strengthen your story, be specific and positive,* not general or negative.

This is *weak:* "I've always looked out for the interests of the company. I've never been late and I've never been absent."

This is *strong:* "When they assigned me to machine Number 328, I was told that the required output was 500 per hour. After two weeks at that rate, I made a jig at home and brought

43

it into the plant and put it on the machine. This increased the output to 750 per hour, with no greater effort on my part. Ever since then, I've been operating at the 750-per-hour rate, with no increase in pay."

HOW TO SELL THE STRONG, SILENT TYPE

Sometimes you'll interview a prospect of the "strong, silent" type. He'll sit and listen to your story. And when you try for commitments he'll give you no response, not even a nod of his head. In such a case you should not make an issue of each commitment. Nor should you stop asking your committing questions.

This type of prospect prides himself on his poker face. He's sure that he's not letting you know what he's thinking. As you ask the committing questions, however, agreement frequently runs through his mind. "This man is right on that point," he's thinking, "but I'm not going to give him the advantage of letting him know that I agree with him."

With certain types of the strong, silent prospect it's safe to answer for them, as in the following example: "Mr. Justin, can you see the benefit of dealing with a large, well-financed, long-established distributor such as ourselves, rather than with some unknown concern who may be here today and gone tomorrow? As experienced as you are, I'm sure you can."

The important thing to remember is to try for several commitments—*whether the prospect answers or not*. When you've secured a minimum of three commitments from the prospect (or when you've asked for six commitments if the prospect is the silent type), as a general rule you are ready to ask for the order. You will be surprised at how many you get.

In using committing questions, it's best to ask them concerning your *exclusive sales features,* or the *prospect's need* for your product, or the *benefits* it will bring him. If all other means fail, then ask, "Why don't you buy my product now?"

HOW A REAL ESTATE SALESMAN
CAN USE QUESTIONS

The real estate salesman who isn't familiar with the importance of asking committing questions might make statements such as the following when trying to sell an old house:

"Beautiful trees!" "Notice that the house has been newly painted and papered. You can move right in without spending a cent on fixing it up." "A lovely shaded street."

After he has read this chapter, the real estate salesman should change these statements into committing questions—retaining the potent language but intensifying its effect immeasurably by putting it in the form of queries rather than positive statements. There's no mystery or magic in it. It's simply putting your strong statements into the form of questions to which the prospect is almost sure to agree.

"Beautiful trees" then becomes "Beautiful trees, aren't they?" "Notice that the house has been newly painted and papered. You can move right in without spending a cent on fixing it up," develops into "With the house newly painted and papered, you can move right in without spending a cent on fixing it up, can't you?" "A lovely shaded street" changes into "A lovely shaded street, isn't it?"

Do you see that the salesman has obtained three commitments and has raised the prospect's buying temperature? Nothing to it, is there? *You* can do that, can't you?

HOW A LIFE INSURANCE SALESMAN CAN USE QUESTIONS

As another example, consider how the productive life insurance salesman introduces one of those ingenious policies that seem to fill almost all the requirements of today's tax-burdened existence. He doesn't say to his prospect, "I've a policy that will provide for your son's college education, give you a retirement annuity, and protect your wife and son." Instead, he asks, "You want your son to go to college, don't you? And you want to be sure your wife and son are protected in case your income ceases, don't you? And you'd like to have a retirement income when you finally live to that ripe old age, wouldn't you?"

Ask for the Order After Summary and Commitments

After you've given your sales story, ask the committing questions. Then summarize the advantages you have established and try for a commitment as you enumerate each point.

When you've obtained three or more commitments in this manner, place the order and a pen before the prospect and say, "Why don't you sign this right now?" If he doesn't sign, summarize once more: "You like the following features in our air conditioner: the depth of the coil, the sturdy cabinet construction, and the compact size. Don't you?"

If you must do a complete selling job—getting an appointment with a prospect, getting him to listen to you, finding out what motivates him, telling your sales story, demonstrating, quoting prices, handling the key objection, meeting competition, asking for the order, and obtaining follow-up sales commitments—it is necessary to obtain a minimum of nine commitments in making a sale. However, that many oral commitments need not be obtained in all cases. Some prospects are ready to buy when you first see them, and therefore only one commitment is necessary—and that is the one to get the order. More typically, only three commitments are necessary to make a sale to most prospects. However, it is up to you to detect which, and how many, commitments will lead to a sale.

SUMMARY THOUGHT-PROVOKERS

A summary of this chapter on "Using Committing Questions" should once more remind you to:

Find out why prospects don't buy

Use questions to improve your selling effectiveness

Let the prospect be the judge

Adjust your selling techniques to handle difficult types of prospects

Get plenty of commitments.

That's all there is to it!

In the next chapter—"Closing the Sale"—you'll see that there's no mystery to closing either.

KEY REVIEW POINTS FOR SELF-IMPROVEMENT

Why do you need several commitments to make a sale?

What are two advantages of obtaining commitments?

When you're interviewing the "strong, silent" prospect, how do you handle commitments?

How do you handle the prospect who says he'll buy if you'll provide him with X—— (something unusual)?

What's the simplest way of obtaining a commitment?

Why should strong statements be made in the form of questions?

Think of some other committing words, in addition to *understand, like, appreciate,* and *owe.*

Why is it better not to say "I'll *convince* you . . ."?

What's an easy way of changing a strong statement into a stronger committing question?

Put more **sell**
into your **tell**

Chapter 5

Closing the Sale

You close the sale, the prospect won't
Know **when** to close and **how** to close
"Do's" and **"Don'ts"** in closing
Add to your **store of closes**
Special **"closing"** remarks
Importance of **leaving**—not being **"left"**

SOMETIMES (but only rarely) the prospect will close the sale himself, if you've developed a good story and have obtained several commitments, as suggested in Chapter 4. Without further action on your part he'll say, "All right, I'm sold. Get out the order so that I can sign it," or, "I'll take it."

Most sales, however, are not made in this manner. If you wait for the prospect to tell you to sign him up or close him, you'll miss ninety-nine out of each hundred sales that you should have made. You must consciously and actively do the closing.

Remember, the salesman makes the close. It isn't enough simply to develop a good story and to get commitments.

Recognize the Time to Close

Some salesmen who work by intuition and rely on various signs and signals from the prospect have difficulty in explaining how to recognize the closing time. Actually, there's no mystery at all about the right time to close. Books have been written by sales "experts" on the art of closing, which is one of the simpler parts of selling. Many of these experts branch off into psychology and the use of five or seven different types of closes. Instead of simplifying selling and making it easy, they may complicate it and make it difficult.

The right time to close is *when the prospect is sold*. He is sold when you're far enough in your story and sales demonstration to have obtained from him a *sufficient number of commitments*. Can you count to three? Then you can tell whether the prospect is ready to close. It is often as simple as that!

CASE ILLUSTRATION OF DETECTING THE TIME TO CLOSE

To illustrate, let's suppose you are selling electrical appliances and a husband and wife have come into the store to look at freezers. By plan and intent, you have so far obtained at least three of the following commitments while you've been developing your sales demonstration:

"Yes, I like the upright freezer."

"The color matches my stove and other equipment."

"The shape fits into the space I have."

"It is the size I want."

"It is the same make as my refrigerator."

"The allowance you mention for our old freezer brings down the price."

The husband then says, "This is the freezer you think will be adequate for our needs?"

At this point, shouldn't you ask for the order?

If the prospect won't buy after having given the minimum of three commitments, usually you have still more selling points to demonstrate, with more commitments to follow— so don't pressure the prospect too much, but return to your basic selling formula.

Keep in mind that prospects don't rush up to you and blurt out voluntarily such statements as those listed above. You must deliberately ask for them by developing a good story and asking committing questions, as has previously been emphasized.

Close in the Right Manner

REPEATING THE PROSPECT'S QUESTION GAINS ACCEPTANCE

Sometimes, at an advanced point in your presentation, the prospect will turn toward his wife and ask, "What do *you* think?" or, "You'd like to have one of these, wouldn't you?"

This usually means that *he* is closed. If you can do it diplomatically, without appearing to pressure the wife, a good idea is to ask her a question before she can answer her husband. *That question should be one that you're sure she'll answer the way you desire.* Perhaps she has already expressed some favorable opinion. Then all you need do is to repeat her remark in the form of a question, such as, "The money-saving feature and the freedom from shopping pressure are both well worth while, aren't they, Mrs. Page?"

When she replies Yes to this question, then say as a close, "Then you are satisfied this is what you want."

If the prospect, after hearing a considerable portion of your presentation and after having given commitments, asks, "How much down payment do you want?" then say, "Mr. Page, how much down payment can you handle?"

Answer this question *by placing a pen and the order form in his hands* as you say, "What amount would be convenient for you, Mr. Page—$300? $200? $100? $50? Put your name right there, sir, because you can make just about any down payment that you choose."

Certain questions from the prospect are buying-interest signals. If the prospect, after having given several commitments, asks any questions such as—"When can you install this?" "May I buy it on the budget plan?" or "Will your unit fit into the utility room?"—it is frequently an indication of a readiness to buy.

Remember the suggestion made in Chapter 4 that the silent prospect could be giving you silent commitments. You've been telling your story and trying for commitments at suitable places. He has remained silent. If you have given several reasons for buying your product (with appropriate demonstration and explanation), *and if you've tried for at least six or more commitments,* you can still attempt to close.

Don't forget to *try for* a close, either after obtaining several commitments or—in the case of the silent prospect—after asking for commitments at appropriate intervals.

There's a difference between selling low-priced "impulse" merchandise in a store and selling in a home, office, or plant. In the store, after the prospect is shown two or three different styles or models or colors of the low-priced merchandise he requests, his choice may be indicated by, "I'll take that one."

If in his home, office, or plant you wait for him to say, "All right, I'll take it; you can write up the order," sometimes he'll say it. But you'll miss many additional sales that you might make if you wait hopefully for this big—and relatively rare—commitment. Remember that you, the salesman, must assist the prospect to arrive at a favorable Yes decision.

To avoid any misunderstanding about selling in a store, when the merchandise sold is upgraded from the low-priced impulse items, the methods described in this book become increasingly effective. The high producers in stores are those salespeople who use them.

USE THE THREE-FOR-ONE IDEA

Bear in mind that three or six or nine small commitments are equal in total and weight to the big commitment that the prospect is willing to buy. In fact, they mean that he *wants* to accept your proposition. Why should you prevent him from fulfilling his desire? You'll be doing him a service at this point if you assist him in making a decision or if you place a pen in his hand and the order in front of him and show him where to put his name.

Another important fact to remember is that billions and billions of dollars' worth of merchandise is sold each year to customers who have *not* said, "I'll take that one" or, "Where is the order? I want to sign it."

When you hand the prospect the order and the pen, you're not making up his mind for him. He's done that for himself when he's given you those three or more previous commitments. What you're doing is giving him the privilege of exercising the decision he has previously declared through his commitments.

Test him; and you'll see that he'll appreciate the opportunity.

Special Pointers When Trying to Close

DON'T PRESSURE OR BEG FOR A CLOSE

You should try for the close at least six times, but *not* in this way:

SALESMAN: "Mr. Brown, put your name right there, please."
MR. BROWN: "No!"

SALESMAN: "Please sign it."

MR. BROWN: "No!"

SALESMAN: "Come on, let's get this over!"

MR. BROWN: "No!"

These are three out of six times, and they are the *wrong* way.

DON'T ASSUME THE FIRST "NO" ALWAYS MEANS "NO"

Too many salesmen try only once for a close. If they're turned down, they conclude the prospect isn't going to buy, and they slink out whipped. It's a big surprise to them to find on their next visit that the prospect has bought a competitive brand from a salesman who really *sold* him.

IMPORTANCE OF THE FIRST CLOSING ATTEMPT

Your first attempt to close should be made after you've obtained at least three commitments. It's a test close. Don't wait until you're *sure* the prospect will sign before trying for the order. Make your first trial to find out how you're progressing and how far away you are from a close. If you wait until you're SURE before trying for the close, you'll talk beyond the closing point in many sales and lose orders that you otherwise would obtain. And often you'll be pleasantly surprised by having the prospect sign on the test close.

TRY TO CLOSE AGAIN AFTER A COMMITMENT ON AN ADDITIONAL FEATURE

If the attempted test close doesn't produce the order, make sure that you have been, and are, developing a good story and getting commitments. Summarize what you've already gone over and get recommitments. Then add the demonstration and explanation of one or two additional selling features and get more commitments. After each additional feature (with its attendant commitments) try again for the order.

SUMMARIZE AND THEN CLOSE

Sometimes the prospect, of his own accord, will tell you his reason for refusing to sign. But he doesn't always mean what he says.

For example, "I want some time to think this over" usually

means that you haven't sold him. If you don't put forth re-doubled efforts at this point to SELL him, you're apt to lose the order entirely. Perhaps at this juncture, if you mentally check over your sales presentation, you'll realize that you haven't been asking committing questions while you've been developing your sales presentation. If this is true, summarize the important features of the sales story that you've already given. As you do this, be sure to try for commitments on each of them.

HOW TO HANDLE THE ANSWER, "I'LL THINK IT OVER"

After this summary you may make another attempt to close, and perhaps the prospect still repeats doggedly, "I want some time to think this over." Then ask, "What do you want to think over?"

You can then test the following reply on him (if your sales presentation has been in his home and his wife has been present): "Mr. Roberts, you've said that you like the exclusive features of our home laundry machine and its many advantages. When you ask for time to think it over, don't you really mean you want some privacy to discuss the financial aspect with your wife? I know that in my house my wife handles our budget. So before making any purchase of this sort, she and I always talk it over to see if we can fit it into our budget. And I think that most people do that. Is that what you have in mind, Mr. Roberts?"

Frequently he'll reply with grateful relief, "Yes, that's what I mean."

If you receive this answer, make an excuse to leave the room (literature from your car or measurements in the basement, for example) and say, "I need another piece of literature from my car. While I'm getting it, you talk this over and do your figuring. After all, your budget and my budget won't be any different three or four days from now than they are tonight, will they? The advantage of your talking it over while I'm available is that if some question comes up in regard to features or terms or payments, I'm here to give you the correct informa-tion, so that you can make up your minds in a sound manner."

This method is sometimes effective. You should remember,

however, that if it were possible to devise the exact statement that will work in *every* instance, selling would be simply a matter of memorizing and elocution.

PROVIDE FOR ANOTHER CHANCE TO
ASK FOR THE ORDER

A question that has been used with good results for many years is, "Do you mind telling me why you want to wait, Mr. Roberts?" You can ask this question when the prospect hasn't decided to buy and hasn't indicated his reason for refusing to do so. If he gives you a frank answer, the clue you obtain may help you in determining the direction of the rest of that particular sales presentation. Often, after answering and overcoming his objection, you'll find that he has one or more additional reasons for not buying. If you can satisfy him and overcome his real reasons for refusing to buy, you should proceed once more with attempts to close.

Have a Repertoire of Closes

Men who've never sold before and who are trying to learn the technique of selling frequently ask, "What shall I say to close them? What are the exact words to use?" From the phrases the old-timers give him in reply, he chooses the one that appears most appropriate for the individual prospect.

Most salesmen, whether they're experienced or inexperienced, are glad to add to their store of closes. Here are several examples that have been productive in various lines.

Don't forget that they're to be used *after* you've obtained sufficient commitments to indicate that the prospect is probably ready to sign. It's the prior commitments that have brought the prospect up to the closing point, you hope and believe. There's no magic in the questions given below. The answer you get to any of them simply enables you to confirm your judgment that the prospect is ready and willing to sign the order. These questions, then, are merely indicators that enable you to proceed confidently with the writing and the confirmation of the order.

"Will installation next Wednesday or next Friday be more convenient?"

"Shall we put you down for one hundred containers each on

54

March first, April first, and May first, or two hundred containers each on the same dates?" or possibly, "How would you want to schedule your shipments?"

"Do you want to pay cash, or would you rather budget this purchase with monthly payments?"

"Will it be satisfactory if we place the unit between these two windows, or would you rather have it in the corner?"

"Will a $300 down payment be convenient for you, or would a different amount suit you better?"

"Will $18.53 a month for thirty-six months fit into your budget, or would you rather make it smaller?"

"Do you mind if I borrow that magazine to put on the table? I don't want to harm the surface while I write on it."

"Which do you want, the two-tone or the solid-color model?"

"You'll want the radio and heater included, won't you?"

"Would quarterly payments of $400 each be convenient for you, or would you rather increase them?"

"Have you any further questions?"

"Have I made everything clear to you?"

"Press hard! There are three carbons." (After you've handed the prospect a ball-point pen or an indelible pencil.)

Reread the closes given above and notice that they're straightforward. You don't need to classify prospects to use them; there's no psychology, phrenology, or mysticism involved.

All that you need do before using them is to be sure that you're far enough along in your sales presentation to have tried for at least three commitments.

ALTERNATE-QUESTION METHOD

Note that almost every one of the thirteen closes above is phrased for an alternate answer—"Do you want this or that?" "Deliver Tuesday or Friday?" and so on. Either way the prospect answers, you have a sale.

Of course, although it is difficult for him to do so, he *can* surprise you and answer, "I don't want either this or that." Or, "Don't deliver either Tuesday or Friday. Don't deliver at all!"

However, if you've been developing a good story and have been *obtaining commitments* as you've progressed, you'll find that the alternate-question method will work very satisfactorily for you in most cases.

Don't make one mistake frequently made by the born salesman. He often feels that there's magic in certain closing words and is lost when they don't bear fruit. Nonsense! The magic —if any—lies in the *strength* and the *number of commitments* you've previously obtained. If you have enough commitments, all you need to do is to ask for the order.

After you've asked any of the preceding closing questions (or some similar question) and received from the prospect the answer you desire, don't say another word. Instead, *without speaking,* fill out your order blank and if a signature is necessary hand the order blank and the pen to the prospect for signature. If he isn't sitting where he can readily sign, either give him a magazine to write on or invite him over to the table or desk where you've been working.

You'll find it better, however, to have him in a writing position from the very beginning of your presentation, rather than to wait for the end, when he may protest. Before starting your presentation, you can get him seated by explaining that you have some pictures and charts for him to see and that it will be more comfortable for him at the table or desk you indicate.

Presentation to Two or More Prospects

Sometimes you have to make your presentation to more than one person at a time (husband and wife, members of a committee, members of a partnership, etc.). When you have this situation, always put *all* of them on your right or *all* of them on your left—that is, all of them in one group and in one direction from you. If they're divided, you'll be swiveling your head from side to side, and frequently one or the other of the prospects will miss some of the points you're trying to make. Also, should they be split, they would be able to flash signals to one another that you'll be unable to intercept.

When you're selling to Mr. and Mrs. Stone a community item such as an automobile, or a home improvement such as air conditioning, you must be sure to include the lady in your sales presentation. Direct your demonstrations and your committing questions to her as well as to her husband. Then, when you're closing, you'll know whether or not she's on your team.

Otherwise it may happen that, just as Mr. Stone is about to put his name on the order, Mrs. Stone bursts forth with, "John! You aren't actually *buying* one of these, are you?" or some other sales-killing remark.

HOW TO HANDLE A SALES-KILLING REMARK

Assuming that you've included the wife in your sales presentation, you don't let her interruption disturb you in the least. Instead, you chide her as follows, "Mrs. Stone, don't stop your husband! He wants to give *you* the greater health and comfort and well-being that this installation will bring. Don't deprive him of this pleasure."

The wording can be changed to fit conditions, but the idea must be made plain to the lady that her husband is doing it for *her*. Nine times out of ten this clears the atmosphere instantly and the close proceeds smoothly.

There may be times when, as you attempt to close, the prospect says, "Hey, wait a minute! I didn't say I was going to *buy* one of these things."

You can try an answer something like this: "You're right, Mr. Stone. But you *did* suggest that you wanted this for your wife. So why don't you decide now, and you will both be glad now and later that you've made this decision."

Important Closing Reminders for You

THE CLOSE IS A DEFINITE STEP IN ANY SALE

Always bear in mind that, when you bring the prospect up to 212° boiling, he won't necessarily drop like ripe fruit into your extended hand. Prodding and activity on your part are still required to secure the close.

Even though he may resist and protest somewhat, you'll find that to close the prospect while he's hot requires less expenditure of energy on your part than if you wait until another visit to move into the close. This is logical, because between the first and second visits he'll have had plenty of opportunity to cool off. On the second call you'll have to bring him up to the same temperature as on the first call. After that, you still must take him through the closing process.

TRY FOR A CLOSE SEVERAL TIMES

So, when the prospect is ready, try for the close—not once, but several times. If you have difficulty, make a quick mental check of your activity up to this point. Correct any omissions or weaknesses in your presentation, and try again and again if necessary for the close.

If your attempts at closing take too much time, your prospect may tend to cool somewhat from that highly desirable 212°. To prevent this, you should intersperse your close with frequent reminders of and recommitments on:

Step 1. Reasons for buying this particular type of equipment.
Step 2. Reasons for buying your brand rather than another.
Step 3. Reasons for buying now.

REPETITION CAN BE EFFECTIVE

Even though he's heard these facts a short time before, they will stand repetition. Human memory is frequently fallible and usually weak. To avoid monotony you can rephrase them or otherwise alter them slightly. And of course you should greatly shorten the explanations and demonstrations when you repeat them.

In selling, hit hard with your heaviest weapons. Throw your Sunday punch! Forcefully and intelligently, try for the order.

DEVELOP SALES RESERVES

Maintain reserves for possible follow-up calls. These reserves should be established without weakening your original sales presentation. For example, they might consist of a visit to customers or to your showroom. Or they may be the story of the evolution of your type of equipment. Or they may be the presentation of a portfolio of users' testimonial letters. These are given as examples. You can think of others.

For example, Edward J. Hegarty suggests the following ideas for holding something up your sleeve:

"A story of performance; i.e., how another customer has used your product or service

"A testimonial letter from a nearby customer

"A list of users

"A list showing how many years you have been doing business with various different customers

"A photograph of a new plant built because of your own company's growth

"A clarification of the action you want

"A big build-up on your best benefit."*

You should maintain reserves so that on each return call you can freshen your presentation by adding something new. In this way you'll refrain from becoming dull and boring to the prospect.

If you've built your sales presentation by choosing three or four outstanding exclusive sales features of your product for explanation and demonstration, this should leave you with many less-important features to hold in reserve. In this connection it's well to remember that what may appear unimportant to you may carry great weight with the prospect. This may be either because a certain idea has unusual appeal to him, or because a competitor may have built up disproportionately the value of this minor feature in the prospect's mind.

ASSIST PROSPECTS IN MAKING A BUYING DECISION

It is true that the salesman must ask for the order in every possible way, but it should be emphasized and remembered that the decision or sale must be made by the buyer. The role of the salesman should be to assist the prospect to make such a decision.

Of course, you may not get the order on your first call on a prospect. In such cases, return or follow-up calls become necessary. Chapter 11 tells how to make return calls productive.

Watch Your Cue to Leave

As soon as possible after you've got the name on the order, put your papers into your brief case and leave. Many sales are lost—after the signing of the order—because the salesman remains and chats too long with the customer.

In some cases ideas come up during post-closing conversations that cause the prospect to ask for delay until the matter in question can be decided.

In other cases, a friend or relative drops in to see the customer while the salesman is still present. A conversation similar to the following may develop in such circumstances:

* Edward J. Hegarty, "How Good Are Your Clinchers," *American Salesman*, February, 1958, pp. 17–22.

CUSTOMER (to visitor): "Jim, look at this food freezer I've just bought!" (Shows him a picture.)

JIM: "Bob, come into the next room a minute."

JIM (out of earshot, in the next room): "Don't you know my brother is in that business? He can save you money. Why don't you see what he can do for you?"

CUSTOMER (?) (to salesman upon returning to room): "Hold up that order, will you? Something has just come up that may prevent my buying."

In both cases mentioned, you'll see that the *customer* reverts to his former status of being simply a *prospect*.

So—get out when you have the order. If it's early, you can tell the customer that you have to make another call. If it's late, you can tell him that it's long past time for you to be on your way.

The salesman of home specialties is frequently invited by the purchaser to celebrate the sale with some refreshments. The wise move is to decline to do so but to ask for a rain check, to be cashed when the equipment has been delivered.

It's hazardous to stay and visit with the customer after the order has been signed and before the delivery has been made. DON'T DO IT!

WHEN YOU LEAVE, SAY "THANK YOU"

A buyer likes to do business with a salesman courteous enough to thank him. Even if you don't get an order, try to find something for which you can thank the prospect. At least you can thank him for giving you permission to make your presentation. A "thank you" when you leave may be the opening for another interview.*

KEY REVIEW POINTS FOR SELF-IMPROVEMENT

Who does the closing?

When is the right time to close?

How can you tell when this time is at hand?

Does the prospect sometimes give you additional indicators that he is ready to close?

* Charles L. Lapp, "The Over-all Impression Counts," *Paper Sales,* December, 1957, pp. 24–25.

Give some examples of closing indicators.

Should you wait for the prospect to say, "All right, I'll take it. You can write up the order."?

When does the prospect make up his mind that he wants your merchandise and is willing to buy it?

Why should you try for the close at least six times?

What steps should you take if your attempted test close doesn't produce the order?

When the prospect says, "I want some time in which to think this over," what does this usually mean?

At what point in your sales presentation should you attempt to close?

Are there any MAGIC closing words?

What is the advantage of "alternate" closing questions?

When you're selling to more than one prospect at a time, where should you seat them?

Should you direct your sales demonstration to only one member of a team or group of prospects, or to all of them?

After you've brought the prospect up to 212°, what should you do with him?

If your prospect tends to cool off because of interruptions or time lapse or other reasons, how can you warm him up again?

How can you build selling reserves?

When should you use them?

When may a relatively unimportant feature carry undue weight with a prospect?

Why is it good practice to leave as soon as possible after obtaining the order?

Remember to close
There is no payoff for ¾ or ⅞ selling!

PART II

HOW TO ADD EXPERT TOUCHES TO YOUR SELLING

Chapter 6

Overcoming Objections

> **Eliminate** the negative approaches
> **Tackle** the objections
> **Accentuate** the positive approaches
> **Control** without dominating
> Don't **sell**; help them **buy**
> Follow the **Golden Rule**

SOME SALESMEN, working largely by instinct, antagonize a prospect. In this chapter you'll see how you can acquire the secret of overcoming objections without making enemies. And again, using actual knowledge instead of unreasoning hunches or instinct, you'll have an advantage over other salesmen.

Avoid Negative Approaches

MINIMIZE THE "I'S"; MAXIMIZE THE "YOU'S"

To avoid antagonizing people, soft-pedal "I," "me," "my," and "mine," and instead talk about "you" and "yours." Won't that be more interesting to anyone? Do you think that the average prospect really cares, for example, whether or not *you're* in a contest and his order will give *you* ten points credit toward a trip to Bermuda? What interests him is the benefits *he* and *his* will obtain from your merchandise, isn't it? Perhaps it might save him enough so that *he* could have that trip to Bermuda! Would that interest him more than *your* contest? You know it would!

DON'T "TOP" YOUR PROSPECT

If the prospect describes the merits of his last-year's-model car, don't mention the fact that you drive this year's beauty. If he tells a funny story, don't immediately crowd off his laugh by telling your anecdote, which you think is much funnier. Wait a while. Or, better yet, forget it. Always try to build up the prospect and his possessions and achievements somewhat higher than you and yours. Then you won't "top" him—which everybody resents.

SYMPATHY APPROACHES WIN NO FRIENDS

Many salesmen attempt to use the sympathy, or personal, angle as a sales clincher. Now and then they find a tender-hearted person who responds to this approach. If these tactics are used independently of any other, they usually fail. Couple them with a "personal benefit" factor for the prospect, and they gain in productivity.

"I'm working my way through college" opens the door. "Here are magazines that you will enjoy and that will assist your husband in his work. When you get them, you'll have extra satisfaction from them because you've helped a deserving young man obtain a college education." Notice the personal-benefit factors, to give the prospect sound motivation from *his* point of view.

ARGUE AND LOSE YOUR CHANCE TO MAKE A SALE

Arguing is something else that antagonizes people. If your prospect is antagonistic and you can't get him to relax and come over to your side, you're sure to lose the sale. It's important that you don't offend anyone, either about your product or about matters that have nothing to do with your product. Antagonism, once created, nurses itself and endures; it carries over into the sale itself and even beyond it.

Suppose, when you enter an office to sell business furniture, your prospect, Mr. Burton, says, "Boy! What a beautiful day! I'd sure like to be out watching the Giants play today. You know, I believe they're going to win the pennant this year."

Even if you're sure that the Giants haven't a chance and can prove that you're right, don't do so. That would be arguing and it would be harmful. Instead, you can be encouraging and noncommittal and make a reply such as, "I hope you win lots of money on them."

It's been said many times that you can win the argument but you lose the sale. A sale is *not* a debate. If you give the prospect ninety-nine reasons why he should buy and he brings forth only one reason why he should not make the purchase, you can still lose the order. The mere weight of reasons won't always produce the sale for you.

The only time you are justified in arguing is when a prospect challenges your integrity or that of your company.

NEVER LOSE YOUR TEMPER

No matter what the provocation, you should never lose your temper. Losing your temper means that you lose your self-control. And if you've lost your self-control, how can you expect to control the sale?

Loss of temper very often is expensive in dollars and in regrets. You'll say and do things when you are angry that you will later wish you could recall.

All of the above is obvious. What may not be so apparent is the fact that prospects, either intentionally or unintentionally, often do and say things that tend to annoy or antagonize you. You can't afford to allow yourself to be irritated in this manner. Remember to keep a hair-trigger temper in check at all times when you're selling. Maintaining your self-control is essential to productive salesmanship.

Of course this last statement also holds true in idea-selling. Here again you can't afford to lose your temper. If you do, you'll find it costly. Even though the provocation may be great, you *must* retain your self-control in order to retain mastery of the situation.

AN INTERRUPTION ANTAGONIZES

Interrupting is another sure way to antagonize a prospect. Moreover, it is a rude habit to acquire. If the prospect rambles along lengthily about matters extraneous to the sale and time is fleeting, at the first available opportunity say something like this: "That's fascinating. I could listen to you on that topic for hours and hours. But we've gotten a long way from the purpose of this visit, haven't we? Now about my product—aluminum foil . . ."

Even where someone makes a definite misstatement and you feel a compelling urge to correct him, don't interrupt! Wait for a favorable pause and then proceed with utmost caution. Remember that corrections are a form of argument. And arguments antagonize.

DON'T CORRECT A PROSPECT UNLESS NECESSARY

While most misstatements by a prospect do not need correction and can usually be ignored, now and then one will be made that you feel cannot safely be overlooked. If you saw Mr. Carlson, the prospect, last Wednesday, and he says, "When you were here last Tuesday you told me that . . .," don't correct him. What difference does the day make, anyway? Enough to justify antagonizing Mr. Carlson and losing the order?

Where the matter is important enough to demand correction, be very careful and diplomatic. Should Mr. Carlson say, "Last week, when we were discussing the possible purchase of your compressor, we were talking about June first delivery . . ." and you know that he is mistaken and that it was July first delivery, according to your notes made at the time, be cautious!

When you correct a prospect, it's best to assume the blame yourself, even though you're innocent.

You say, "It looks like I pulled a boner, Mr. Carlson, because I wrote down July first delivery. Is June first the date that you want this compressor?"

If he answers "Yes," you try for the big commitment:

"If we can pull a rabbit out of our sleeve and make delivery of our compressor June first, will you give me the order right now?"

If he replies "Yes," you ask, "If I reverse the charges, may I use the telephone and see what we can do for you on this?"

Tackling the Objection

LISTEN BEFORE YOU SPEAK

Should your prospect object to or criticize your product and you don't listen to him, he may become annoyed with you.

It's advisable, therefore, that you inquire *before* you answer. Learn what his objections are before you begin your presentation. By doing this your path will be made smoother and your sales effort will be vastly improved. It's wise to write the prospect's objections on your pad, so that you can be sure to adapt your sales story to cover the point that he has raised. Explain to him what you're doing. He'll like it.

ENCOURAGE THE PROSPECT TO TALK

How can you learn these pertinent objections? One way is by encouraging the prospect to talk. Another way is by asking him appropriate questions. For this purpose you can use queries similar to the following:

"I suppose, Mr. Burton, you've been giving a lot of thought to this installation?"

"Do you have any particular objection to equipment of this type?"

"Is there any special feature about this kind of equipment that worries or annoys you?"

"What do you consider the biggest problem in its installation?"

"Is there any particular type of equipment in this field that appeals to you strongly? . . . Why does that appeal to you?"

"Have you ever considered streamlining the handling of incoming orders to save time and money?"

But be careful to prevent such an inquiry from resembling a cross-examination. If you "put the prospect in the witness chair" with a series of annoying questions, you're sure to antagonize him. At that point, bid the sale farewell.

ASK QUESTIONS WITH A PURPOSE

It's a good practice to try to obtain the prospect's objections *before* you tell your story. Otherwise you may neglect to answer them in your presentation. This neglect usually means a lost sale, for the prospect harbors any real objections and nurses them until they assume overwhelming weight. Interspersed during your sales presentation, you should ask additional questions, to assure agreement or to bring out any further objections.

A query now and then during the sale, such as one of the following, may well be productive:

"I trust you agree with that?"

"Do you see anything against that?"

"Do you have any objections to that?"

"Have I made myself clear?"

"Do you have any further objections?"

FIND THE KEY OBJECTION

Expert salesmen find out what is the key objection and concentrate their selling points on it. But it's frequently difficult to determine the key objection. Prospects have a habit of stating several reasons why they won't buy, none of which is the true reason. After you've answered these objections satisfactorily and have won the prospect over to your side, then try for the order. If you don't get it and you're satisfied that your sales technique is not to blame, you can be reasonably sure that the prospect has another objection—the real reason (known as the key objection) that prevents your making the sale.

SAMPLE KEY QUESTIONS TO FIND HIDDEN OBJECTIONS:

"Mr. Underwood, do you have any objection to telling me what is standing between you and me and the order?"

"Mr. Johnson, is there any reason why we can't do business right now?"

"Mr. Hewitt, have I made everything clear? Is there something else that you'd like explained?"

"Mr. Dunbar, is there some reason why you think this drill press might not give you the results you want?"

RESTATE THE PROSPECT'S OBJECTION

When you've obtained an objection from the prospect, it's helpful to restate it in your own words.

Perhaps, for example, you're trying to sell insurance. The prospect says, "I'm loaded. I can't afford any more insurance."

Before answering the objection it's best to repeat it, changing it somewhat to let the prospect know that you comprehend exactly what he means. This frees his mind and heads off resentment.

If you don't do this, too often the prospect is thinking his own thoughts instead of listening to your carefully-worked-out plan to show him where and how he can gather together the funds to pay for the insurance. They frequently run like this: "I wonder if this guy understood me. To be sure, he said he had something that would make paying practicable, even for me. But did he grasp the fact that I am now really carrying all the insurance that I can handle?"

So clear his mind, block off possible resentment, and secure his attention to your presentation by rephrasing his objections in your own words. You might say, at the start, "I imagine you mean, Mr. Beck, that after paying your running expenses in these days of high prices, and after taking care of payments on this nice home of yours, and after putting a little into your savings account, you don't have a great deal left over for adding to your insurance. Is that right?"

An experienced insurance man will notice that an affirmative answer to this provides the salesman with two avenues to the sale: (1) providing a home clear of mortgage in case of the prospect's death; and (2) insurance as a type of savings PLUS.

ORIENT YOUR STORY TO THE KEY OBJECTION

When the key objection is found, you should center your sales story on it. This doesn't mean that you should concentrate on it to the exclusion of everything else. It *does* mean that you should tell your regular sales story, but shape it so that each selling point is directed to answer the key objection.

Probably the commonest and most formidable key objection is, "I can't afford it," or, "I haven't the money." It's usually a waste of time to give your sales presentation in such a case if the prospect is actually telling the truth. You could, instead, be using your time to better advantage by presenting the story of your product to someone able to buy. But how can you tell whether or not the prospect *can* afford your product?

Here's a simple method that has solved the problem countless times. Suppose you're trying to sell a room air conditioner for $295. The prospect declares, "I can't afford it. I haven't the money."

Say something like this to him: "Mr. Seward, I'm not making you an offer, but I *do* have something in the back of my mind. To help me, and to help you, I wonder if you'd be willing to answer a hypothetical question."

To this he'll usually answer Yes.

Then: "Suppose—just suppose—that, instead of $295 for this room conditioner I could let you have it for a total price of $50; would you be interested? This $50 would not be a down payment but would be the full price. Would you buy it if I could sell it to you for $50?"

If he says Yes, you know that he isn't so hard pressed financially as he has claimed. He has at least $50 of spendable money. With a Yes from him at this point, you should be ready for a strong follow-up.

Something of this nature may be effective: "As I said, I don't claim to be able to let you have this $295 air conditioner for $50. But I may surprise you and come so close to doing it that you'll hardly notice the difference. Here's the way we do it. You give us the $50 and we'll install the air conditioner. Then you give us $8.06 a month for thirty-six months, while you're getting the benefits of air conditioning. Actually, if you take into consideration the more restful sleep, the freedom from hay fever you'll have, and the relief to your heart during hot, humid weather, and put a value on these savings, you'll find that they come to much more than $8.06 a month, won't you? Have you ever felt drowsy at work and wished that you'd had a good sleep the previous night? Isn't it worth money to you to be alert and to do better work in your business? Can you see that this $50 outlay not only gives you greater comfort and enjoyment and health and a longer life, but also actually saves money for you, both in better health and in increased productivity? So that, to all intents and purposes, all you're paying for additional years of comfort and health and increased productivity is $50, isn't it? The savings in your health budget and the increased productivity at work can easily make up the $8.06 monthly payments, can't they?"

Develop the Positive Approaches

RELATE YOUR SALES STORY TO THE PROSPECT'S POINT OF VIEW

Prospects are frequently reluctant to place their confidence in a salesman's advice. If you can overcome this understandable hesitation, the results are well worth the effort you've put forth. You're on the road to making both a sale and a friend.

Not only in selling products or services, but also in idea-selling (such as trying for a raise or applying for a position), you'll usually make much more progress by helping the prospect to buy than by trying to sell him. That is, you visualize yourself in his place and make your presentation from his point of view.

Here is an example of this attitude: "Mr. Irwin, I've a lot of confidence in this company and in the way it's run. If I didn't, I wouldn't work for it. I believe that the management tries to pay its workers fairly and to reward extra effort. But you've a great many other problems to consider besides that of remuneration of employees. Sometimes it's possible that news of achievement may be delayed or sidetracked in reaching you. I'm not sure whether you know it, but I'm the man who suggested and installed cycle billing here. I've waited six months to speak to you about it, until the pattern of results would become plain. I wanted to be sure that our ratio of collections each month would continue, and actually it has gone up 1.7 per cent. Although I can't claim that this is due to cycle billing, I do feel safe in concluding that cycle billing hasn't harmed our collection ratio. The big advantage, Mr. Irwin, is in the financial saving. Have you seen the figures, Mr. Irwin? Did you know that we've saved $8,000 a year of overtime payments in my department by eliminating the end-of-month rush to get out statements?"

The boss isn't nearly so interested in why you need more money as in what you've done to earn and save money for the company. List two or three specific accomplishments that have proved profitable. Let him see how much additional profit you've earned for the company. But it won't do you much good to stress how hard it is to get along on your present level of income. He's probably having similar trouble himself, even though his income is considerably greater than yours.

USE ASSURANCE PHRASES

How do you get people on your team when they make antagonistic remarks? Here are some assurance phrases that have been used successfully:

"I don't blame you for feeling that way, Mr. Norris. If I were in your shoes, I'd feel the same way myself."

"You're absolutely right, Mr. Norris. Gas pilots *have* snuffed out and filled the house with gas. But that can't happen with our unit. I must have overlooked describing our thermal electric pilot control. As soon as the pilot goes off in our unit, this bar chills and shrinks, actuating a positive electric cutoff valve. You'd feel safe with its never failing action, wouldn't you?"

"That's a very important point you've just made, Mr. Norris. Do you think the fact that we have only one moving part, with self-oiling lubrication, would tend to solve that problem?" (Note that here you've put your answer to his objection in the form of a question, so as to obtain an agreeing commitment.)

"That's true, Mr. Norris. That radiation shield gave our engineering department one of their biggest problems. This is how they licked it."

"That's a very intelligent question, Mr. Norris. I can see that you've gone into this subject most thoroughly. Therefore you're particularly well qualified to appreciate this expansion valve of ours, which eliminates that condition."

"I don't blame you for feeling that way, Mr. Norris. Many people feel the same as you do." (This is a noncommital remark that can be used where you don't agree with the prospect and where the subject isn't of vital importance to the sale.)

"You must have a particular reason for feeling that way. Would you be willing to tell me about it?"

You'll notice that in the preceding examples you agree with the prospect and then attempt to inform him rather than to argue with him.

CONDUCT A TWO-WAY CONVERSATION

The sales presentation shouldn't be a monologue by you, with the prospect silent, never saying a word. Some people want to talk. If they're not allowed to do so, they take offense. You should encourage the prospect to participate in the sale. Try to guide his conversation so that it remains largely on the subject of the product. Well-put questions at intervals usually aid the prospect to express himself. They can be simple ones,

71

such as, "Do you have any questions?" or, "Do I make myself clear?"

Keep your eyes on the prospect, and if he starts to speak, stop talking—in the middle of a sentence if necessary—and ask, "Yes, Mr. Ryan? Have you a comment?"

By encouraging the prospect to ask questions, you make the opportunity of clarifying any troublesome points. Moreover, if you can persuade him to ask questions, that's one way of obtaining his participation in the sale. His inquiries will also provide insight into his thoughts.

Don't forget, therefore, to encourage the prospect to ask questions and express ideas during your sales presentation.

ADDITIONAL POSSIBILITIES FOR
PROSPECT PARTICIPATION

Other types of prospect participation are: having him help with the measuring when you make a survey in his home; having him handle and examine your demonstration model (put it into his hands); having him look at the pictures with you, as well as charts and diagrams in your sales presentation portfolio; having him check your figuring when you arrive at the monthly payments he's to make. An excellent form of participation when selling to homeowners is to encourage their children to operate your demonstration model: "Look, it's so simple a child can operate it."

Control, Not Dominate the Sales Interview

To give a good sales demonstration, you must control and manage the interview. Yet if you openly dominate the prospect you'll antagonize him. Do *you* like to be bossed around? No? Well, neither does the prospect. Therefore, do your interview-managing unobtrusively and without open domination. Try to guide or lead the prospect into the paths you want him to follow rather than to force him there.

Always Help the Prospect Buy

Some people resent being sold. This is particularly true if they feel they're being forced or pushed into a sale. They put up their guard against salesmen who do this, and they try to repel such efforts. So, to avoid antagonizing prospects, don't "sell" them; instead, *help them buy*.

If you sincerely try to imagine yourself in the prospect's shoes and act as his purchasing agent, you'll not only be helping him to buy but you'll find selling more enjoyable and more productive than if you're simply trying to get the order.

Suppose, for example, that you're an automobile salesman. A prospect walks into the showroom and says to you, "I'd like to buy an automobile."

Answer No. 1: "And I'll be glad to sell you one." (Salesman's viewpoint emphasized.)

Answer No. 2: "If you'll tell me what you have in mind, I'll do everything I can to help you find just the car you want."

The greater effectiveness of the second reply is obvious.

Adopt the Golden Rule

Perhaps the best way to avoid antagonizing people is to practice the Golden Rule. Treat them as you'd like to be treated. You want others to be friendly and polite to *you*, so of course you'll be friendly and polite to them. You appreciate their interest and helpfulness; in like manner they'll appreciate *your* interest and helpfulness. However, keep in mind that some people prefer a different treatment than you prefer. Naturally, treat people as *they* want to be treated.

You've probably noticed that the practices described in this chapter on "Overcoming Objections" are mostly negative. You may follow all these suggestions and still leave the prospect in a neutral frame of mind. He won't be against you, to be sure, but again, he won't always be actively for you. Also remember, to obtain your maximum output as a salesman, you must ask for the order, as discussed in Chapter 5.

KEY REVIEW POINTS FOR SELF-IMPROVEMENT

Why should you adopt the attitude of acting as the prospect's purchasing agent?

How can you help a prospect buy the right merchandise?

Why should your sales presentation stress "you" and "yours" rather than "me" and "mine"?

Should a sales presentation ever evolve into a debate?

Why should you typically not argue with a prospect?

When may arguing with a customer pay off?

When prospects make antagonistic remarks, how can you get them on your team?

Why should you control your temper when selling?

Why should you keep your self-control when selling?

What may be lost by interrupting a prospect?

What are the advantages of learning the prospect's objections to your type of product *before* you start your sales presentation?

How can you uncover such objections?

Should you ask additional questions during your sales presentation to bring out further objections?

Why should you restate the prospect's objections in your own words?

How can you get the prospect to participate in your sales demonstrations?

Give an example of an invitation to the prospect to ask a question.

Why should you encourage the prospect to ask questions?

Tact and self-control **will win**
the approval of customers

Chapter 7

Handling the Price Shopper

Recognizing the **price shopper**
Changing the **shopper** into the **buyer**
The **effective approach** for price shoppers*
Facts about price **quotations** and price
  competition

THE PRICE shopper is the prospect who takes your time and
accepts your demonstration and listens to your sales story;
then, after he gets your trade-in allowance or your price, he
goes trotting off to three or four other dealers to buy from the
one who gives him the best price. Time after time you do all
the work of selling prospects on your make or brand only to
have them buy from some other dealer or salesman who gives
them a higher trade-in allowance. This chapter covers such
situations to help you develop effective strategies for dealing
with difficult price-oriented prospects.

Changing the Shopper into the Buyer

INITIAL STEPS IN HANDLING THE PRICE SHOPPER

To reduce the number of price shoppers and increase the
number of buyers, follow these five steps:

1. *Kindle the prospect's desire* for the product to overcome
crucial price issue. Therefore be sure to give a good sales
demonstration. To do this, construct a planned sales story
(adhering to the 1–2–3 Formula previously given). Use the
planned sales story. Try for and get at least three commitments
after each major sales point. Also try for commitments after
minor points. By obtaining these major and minor commit-

* Charles L. Lapp, *Successful Selling Strategies*, New York: McGraw-Hill,
1957, pp. 6, 118–120, 254.

ments, you'll be increasing the intensity of the prospect's desire for your product. This desire for ownership will in many cases overshadow and neutralize his thought that he might be able to save some money by getting a better trade-in or a better price elsewhere.

2. *Delay discussion of the trade-in allowance or price,* if possible, until you've raised the prospect's buying temperature by giving a substantial portion of the sales demonstration (and demonstration ride) and obtaining commitments during the process. Many salesmen have a relatively high percentage of price-shopper buyers because they permit themselves to be drawn into the trade-in-allowance contest or a price discussion before they've raised the prospect's buying temperature by an adequate sales demonstration, with commitments. Haven't these salesmen attempted to short-cut? And, in selling, don't short cuts frequently lead to failure? (Unless, as pointed out earlier, a prospect says he wants to be sold in a hurry.)

3. A large financial purchase, such as an automobile, a major appliance, or real estate usually involves *consultation and agreement* between husband and wife. If only one member of the partnership (the wife, for instance) appears, you will of course give your best sales demonstration. At the same time you'll attempt to make a follow-up appointment: "When can Mr. Travers have the experience of driving the car (or looking at the real estate property or the major appliance) for himself?"

4. *Try for a close* when you've progressed far enough in your planned sales demonstration and have obtained sufficient commitments to make you feel that the prospect may be at 212°. Use a further commitment or commitments, such as, "Mr. Walters, you and Mrs. Walters liked that maroon and gray four-door (or you liked the room arrangement of that house) that you saw, didn't you? If I could have that very car (or very house) made ready and available to you in forty-eight hours, are you ready to buy right now?"

If they say No, this means that you haven't sold them. Your next step is to determine the reason by asking the prospect, "Why?" His answer then points to what will be your next course of action. Then you can review some of your major features again, with committing questions. Then add a demonstration of more features, with committing questions. After that, try again for the close.

5. *Review some of the features the prospects liked,* and again obtain commitments. Suppose, however, that you feel that you've given an excellent sales demonstration, and that you've been careful to obtain plenty of commitments, and that you've quoted "$1400 and your car for that beautiful new ——" (or a down payment of $5000 on a house), and the prospects won't sign the order.

SALES TECHNIQUE TO TRANSFORM
THE SHOPPER INTO THE BUYER

You then follow through with something like this: "You like the color, the styling, the smart interior, the operating economy—don't you, Mr. and Mrs. Walters? Well, then, we will go ahead and get this car (or this house) ready for you."

You are quite sure that Mr. and Mrs. Walters are thinking of shopping around in an effort to get a better deal. If by deft questioning you can induce them to mention their plan, that's the preferable way of handling it. However, if you're convinced you're right about their desire to shop around, it should be brought to light at this point.

"Is it the matter of the trade-in allowance (or down payment), Mr. and Mrs. Walters?" you can ask, if you have to. "If you'll tell me so frankly, I may be able to help you."

"Well," Mr. Walters may reply, "I like your car (or the house) and you've been most pleasant and most thorough, but we're not millionaires. I do feel that in all fairness to myself and as a matter of good business, I should get the best trade-in deal (or lowest down payment) that I can."

"I don't blame you," you respond; "I might feel the same way myself. I have given you the rock-bottom cash price for this new ——, based on the highest possible trade-in value for your —— sedan; but, Mr. Walters, the rock-bottom cash price for the car you want, in exchange for your —— sedan, is $1400, which is just what I quoted before. We pride ourselves upon our reputation and you can have confidence in us. We have cut our overhead costs of doing business—rent, heat, taxes, advertising, personnel, salaries, etc., without giving less service, but giving more service. All dealers pay the manufacturer the same price for his ————. Your ———— sedan doesn't jump in value just because you spend an hour or two driving it to another dealer's showroom, does it? He has the same costs of doing business that we do, doesn't he? If you should be able to get a lower price than ours, such a dealer has to make it up in some way or other. Once more, allow me to remind you that our company has been in business for forty years because of our fair dealing with customers. Also, we hire only the best mechanics to service your car. Now, if you will allow me to tell our service department to go ahead, we can have your car ready in forty-eight hours, completely serviced."

An Approach for the Price Shopper

It isn't always easy to get the price-shopper prospect to let you give your planned sales presentation. Suppose you're selling air conditioning. What are you going to do when the prospect says, at the very beginning of the interview, "Yes, I'm interested in air conditioning. How much is your three-ton water-cooled unit, set in this office?" You can only answer by quoting the price. He may stop you with, "That's too much money. I'm not going to pay that much."

Or he may jot down your figures on a list and say, "Thanks very much. I have your price, and as soon as I get two more prices I'll be able to make my choice. If I decide on your unit, you'll hear from me."

What should you do then? How can you tell your story to sell your product? Since this prospect's personality is a strong factor, there's no answer that will apply in every individual case. Here, however, is a treatment that has proved effective in a sufficiently high proportion of similar situations to make its consideration worth while.

"You're going at this in a very intelligent manner, Mr. Howard. When you get all these prices listed, you probably won't choose the lowest-priced unit because you're not a price buyer. You know that it doesn't pay to buy cheap, poorly engineered products, and that you usually get just about what you pay for—don't you, Mr. Howard? And you rarely get something for nothing, do you? You'll probably not choose the highest-priced unit either, because you'll figure that some-where somebody is making too much money. So you'll probably pick one of the units in the middle-price range, won't you? Am I right, Mr. Howard?

"As I see it, actually you're not so much interested in whether you buy at the bottom price or at the top price, but what you want to do is to get the greatest value for each dollar that you spend, isn't it? I'm able to make this guess as to what's in your mind because that was the reasoning of our company after we surveyed buyer desires when we took on this line of air-conditioning equipment. We're a long-established company, of good financial standing, and we had our choice of over a dozen lines. Most of them were lower in price than the one we chose. But no other gave as much for the money.

"Only one of the others, for example, was made by a single manufacturer; and that manufacturer didn't have the experience and the stability of the one who makes our equipment. None of the other units was as *sturdily built* as ours [product feature], which will insure long life and freedom from service [benefit makes a selling point]. None of the others was as *quiet* as ours, which is only natural when you consider the strength of our construction and the fact that each part is made for the others in the same factory and it's not assembled on a price basis. Quietness is important to you and your staff, isn't it, Mr. Howard? Only two of the others had *automatic controls* similar to ours, but there again the controls were of a cheaper make and we doubted their effectiveness. None of them showed the same *economy of operation* as ours, which is certainly an advantage as far as long-range cost is concerned."

Here the prospect frequently asks, "Do I get a discount for cash?"

You can answer, "In one sense of the word, yes, because you save $180 of three-year carrying charges from the total budget price if you pay cash. The net cash price to you is $1100. Which way would you rather buy?"

Quoting the Total Price

Expert salesmen often find it feasible not to break down the price. If, for example, you're selling automatic gas heating equipment for a home and the prospect wants a circulating pump installed with the boiler, quote one lump sum as the complete price. Say this: "The price of our equipment, completely installed, including circulating pump, is $975."

Do NOT say, "The price of our equipment, completely installed, is $825. The circulating pump will cost you another $150, so the total will be $975."

Countless sales have been lost because the salesman broke down the price, as in the preceding example. Perhaps the competitive salesman can't offer the same boiler that you do, because you have it exclusively. However, he *can* offer the same circulating pump, and he quotes it to the prospect at only $110 (his cost or possibly a little below cost). Using this price breakdown comparison as a wedge, he doesn't find it difficult to persuade the prospect that his boiler (although actually lighter and not so well constructed) is just as good as yours—even though it too sells at a lower price.

Where you quote a complete price, including the extras, sometimes the prospect asks, "How much additional are you charging for the circulator?"

Here, although you would prefer not to do so, you're forced to break down the price. Your answer could be along these lines: "I'm charging $150, which is our very low price, considering the careful labor, workmanship, material, and engineering we put into its installation. Sometimes other firms quote lower prices by trying to put in some cheap items at cost. We find that they frequently attempt to short-cut with cheap labor, second-rate or even used fittings, etc., in an attempt to salvage a few dollars of profit out of their bad bargain. We don't do that. Everything we give you is first-rate—labor, workmanship, material, and engineering. Isn't it worth the fair amount that we charge?"

Support Your Price Quotations

If you slap your left wrist sharply with your right hand, your wrist stings. If you repeat this action, rubbing your wrist immediately after the slap, the sting isn't noticeable and disappears at once.

Expert salesmen know this. They're careful not to allow a price quotation or other unpleasant bit of information to remain unsupported, exerting its full shock or sting. Instead, they expand their statement with explanatory conversation, thus removing the price sting. Here's an example:

Mr. Blake walks into Mr. Florio's showroom. Mr. Blake says: "Mr. Florio, I understand you're the finest custom tailor in this city."

MR. FLORIO (with too much modesty): "I wouldn't want to say that about myself."

MR. BLAKE: "I'd like to have a good suit. How much are yours?"

MR. FLORIO: "My price for a three-piece suit is $250."

MR. BLAKE: "That price sounds very high. I don't want to spend that much."

MR. FLORIO: "I'm sorry. That's our price."

MR. BLAKE (leaving): "Good-by."

MR. FLORIO: "Good-by."

Actually, Mr. Florio not only is a master tailor, cutter, and designer, but he's also an artist in his profession and takes an artist's pride in his creations. Suppose his expertness in selling approached his skill in tailoring. Then the conversation might have proceeded as given below:

MR. BLAKE: "Mr. Florio, I understand you're the finest custom tailor in this city."

MR. FLORIO: "I'm proud that my many customers think so. And, if you won't think I'm conceited, I'll add that my fellow designing custom tailors must feel that way too, as they've elected me president of both our local association and of the national association of the finest custom tailors in the United States."

MR. BLAKE: "You've a right to feel proud. I'm glad to know you. I'd like to have a good suit. How much are yours?"

MR. FLORIO: "My price for a three-piece suit is $250, which is very modest when you consider that you get not only your choice of the finest of domestic and imported fabrics, but also a garment that fits you when you leave here as well as after you've worn it. Naturally, when I make your clothes, I won't let you walk out of this showroom with one of my suits if it doesn't fit you properly. I've too much pride in my work to do that. Moreover, it would be a bad advertisement for me. And I haven't built my business by bad advertising.

"Another thing I do, Mr. Blake, is to have you come

81

in later, so that I can check the fit of your Florio suits after you've worn them long enough to set to the contours of your body and your activities. Fabrics have a certain amount of 'give' to them. After you've worn a suit for a while, you may have changed its fit by the strain of driving your car, for example. Then, when I see it, I can tell whether your Florio suit fits with the same perfection after it sets to your body as when it first came out of my workrooms. If it doesn't, I know the adjustments that are necessary to make it a suit in which you and I will both take pride and satisfaction.

"You've never before had a Florio suit, Mr. Blake. You're about to have a new and most satisfying knowledge of what the finest in custom tailoring can really mean to you. I congratulate you in advance, Mr. Blake, on the enjoyment and satisfaction you'll obtain from your Florio suit!"

Meeting Competition with a Lower Price

If your product is higher-priced than others, you can try something along the lines of the following:

"It's no secret that you can buy others for less. But ours isn't somewhat higher because we take a bigger margin. If someone offers to put in your equipment without making any money, beware! He's either trying to deceive you, or else he won't stay in business very long—should you ever need service. You have to make money to stay in business.

"In mechanical equipment, such as this trench-digger, Mr. Carter, the cost is made up by the manufacture of the product, its distribution, and its service cost. For someone to sell his product at a lower price than ours, he has to cheapen it somewhere, doesn't he? You're not getting something for nothing, are you? Those dollars aren't just given to you. They're taken out some place, aren't they?—either from the manufacture through lighter, sleazier materials or cheaper, poorer workmanship; or from the distribution through an organization that may be here today and gone tomorrow, and with doubtful parts and service facilities should you ever need them; or from the service itself through low-priced labor and low-priced—or even nonexistent—engineering.

"You usually get just about what you pay for, don't you, Mr. Carter? The lower price simply must be taken out of one or more of these sources. There's no other place to get it, is there? If you're thinking that a lower profit might account for the price reduction, our margin of profit is so narrow that if we should operate without any profit at all, the total resulting reduction in price would by itself not bring our price as low as the Whoosis trench-diggers. We call all competitive makes 'Whoosis,' Mr. Carter, so that we can compare ours with them without condemning any particular make.

"No, Mr. Carter, we haven't attempted to construct a digger that will be the lowest priced *to buy*. Our purpose—in which, I'm happy to say, we've been successful—is to provide you with a digger that has the lowest cost *to own*. This happy result comes about because it hasn't been cheapened or weakened in an attempt to lower the price. You're not buying this digger for just one day's use, are you, Mr. Carter? Don't you think we have the right philosophy when we provide for you a digger whose over-all cost to you, including operation, is the lowest by far? Do you agree with our philosophy when we provide for you a manufacturer and a distributor who are strong and experienced? Doesn't the lowest *cost,* instead of the lowest *price,* appeal to you, Mr. Carter?"

SHAKE THE PROSPECT'S CONFIDENCE
IN A LOW PRICE

Another way to weaken competition is to shake the prospect's confidence in your competitor—if his price is lower. An example follows:

SALESMAN: "You've just told me, Mr. Green, that another salesman has offered you a storage freezer $50 under my price of $350. He claims that his freezer, although lower in price, is just as good as mine. Do you believe this? Don't you usually get just about what you pay for—no more, no less?

MR. GREEN: "Usually."

SALESMAN: "Perhaps he's given you some plausible arguments, and you're inclined to believe he's telling the truth. Yet if the same man had offered to sell you his freezer at $100, $150, $200, or $250 less, trying to assure you that his product is just as good as this one that costs more, somewhere in this range you'd lose confidence in him, because you'd know that such things are impossible and that he's trying to deceive you, wouldn't you?"

MR. GREEN: "Sure I would."

SALESMAN: "Where does his attempt at deception begin, Mr. Green? At $250, $200, $150, $100, or at $50?"

Meeting Competition with a Higher Price

Contrariwise, if it's *your* product that's lower in price than the competition, you must justify this lower price to the prospect in order to maintain his confidence in you. So if your price is lower than the competitors', have some compelling and reassuring reasons for your low price. Two examples follow:

1. SALESMAN: "Mr. Furman, we're trying to get as many units as possible into the hands of customers during the month of June. We've found that each window air conditioner in a customer's home means additional sales to us through 'radiation' business. That is, each user is so enthusiastic that he's glad to send us to his friends. We want to build the biggest summer's business we've ever had. As nearly as we can figure it, without offering this low price we'll sell x units in June. But by offering it, we believe we'll sell at least $2x$ units in June, and the total gross margin on which we operate will still remain the same."

2. SALESMAN: "Mr. Hall, we can give you more for your money than anyone else because we're a chain. The independent store buys in small quantities, through a jobber or wholesaler. We buy direct from the manufacturer in tremendous quantities for our entire chain of stores and save you the middleman's profit."

Selling the Price Shopper Low-Unit-Value Items

Turning now to smaller transactions, in which merchandise in the price range of a television set or a room cooler or a refrigerator is being considered, you may be a mere $50 higher than competition. The odd thing about the prospect is that, whereas he knows that he gets just about what he pays for, he wants to buy the cheaper item with the assurance that it's just as good as yours and he's saving money.

Here you shrink the difference in price by setting up the transaction in its true light.

84

Let's assume that the prospect (Mr. Thomas) has said: "I can save $50 on your price."

SALESMAN: "The same model, from the same manufacturer?"

MR. THOMAS: "No, a different manufacturer."

SALESMAN: "You usually get just about what you pay for, don't you? And you rarely get something for nothing? So you'll pay $50 less and get $50 less in actual value. If that's what you want, I can tell you where you can buy for $75 or $100 less. But I don't advise you to do it. Because you'll be $75 or $100 sorrier, instead of just $50 sorrier. May I ask you a couple of questions, Mr. Thomas, and then you be the judge?"

MR. THOMAS: "Go ahead."

SALESMAN: "Is the manufacturer as strong and experienced and as well known and as well established as ours, in case you should ever need a part? Or was the first time you ever heard of the manufacturer when the salesman offered to sell his merchandise to you on a price basis?"

MR. THOMAS: "I don't know much about the manufacturer."

SALESMAN: "Is this the manufacturer's de luxe Grade A model, or is it his second line, cheapened to cater to the price market? The model that I'm offering you is our de luxe Grade A line."

MR. THOMAS: "I don't know."

SALESMAN: "You realize that this distributor I represent is well established and well rated financially and has been here for a very long time—over twenty years, in fact. If you need service or advice or attention, you don't need to worry, do you, when you buy from us? Do you know as much about the salesman who offers you the cut price?"

MR. THOMAS: "No, I don't."

SALESMAN: "Then why take a chance? Allow me to place your order now. You realize, instead of saving $50, if anything goes wrong, your cut-rate purchase can cost you far more than $50 additional? If you feel our merchandise is fairly priced, when you consider that we have an experienced manufacturer, a dependable distributor, and a quality product that is well engineered, then the only decision necessary before we begin the processing of your purchase is whether you want the equipment shipped by rail or truck."

Never Ask, "How Much Do You Want to Pay?"

The result is usually unfortunate when you ask a price shopper, "How much do you want to pay?" Miss Jo Anne Ketcham, Research Assistant at the Bureau of Business Research at The Ohio State University, makes this observation:

"Price is, to be sure, an important part of any sale, but it is not one of the things that can be gone at directly, in so many words. Even though some customers do not mind being asked what price they want to pay, it is better to have the price come in naturally at the point where the customer asks about it himself.

"If, for instance, you find that he wants to know the price immediately, then on all succeeding items, it may be stated at once."*

Taking the Price Prospect Out of the Market

An exception to the above procedure is those cases where the prospect has asked for some special feature or service. Suppose, for example, that your usual terms are three years to pay, and after you've secured several commitments from him the prospect asks, "Could you give me five years to pay instead of three years?"

Then you can come back with the big question: "If you want to give me the order based on five years to pay, I will submit it for acceptance!"

Should he reply, "You find out whether you can get five years for me and we'll see about it," you probably haven't sold him thoroughly. But should he reply, "Yes, if you'll give me five years to pay I'm ready to sign the order right now," then you proceed as follows:

You start writing the order, based on five years, and you say to the prospect, "I'm filling this out for five years, Mr. King, and I'm going to take it into the office with your signature. I'll try to get it through, and I may be able to. If I don't, it won't be because I haven't tried."

If he protests about giving you the order before you're certain about the five-year period for payment, you can let him know that you're adding a cancellation clause in case the five

* Jo Anne Ketcham, "How to Find Need by Questions," *The Ohio Retail Analyst*, January, 1954, pp. 23–24.

years are unobtainable. If he protests further, you can tell him that the only way you know of to get an exception through is to bring in the order and lay it on the sales manager's desk.

ADVANTAGES OF TAKING A PROSPECT
OUT OF THE MARKET

Should you get the order in this manner, you have wasted one order form in case the management rejects it. That's on the liability side. On the asset side are three advantages:

1. Some way will perhaps be found by the management to put through the order with its unusual clause.
2. You may still have a chance of getting the prospect to sign the standard three-year order, if you have to come back to tell him the five-year terms have been rejected.
3. During the time between the signing and your return call, it's probable that the prospect will be out of circulation, because it's likely he's telling competitive salesmen, "I've already signed an order."

You can put this extra time to use by working out an approach to help shrink the difference in monthly payments on a five-year and a three-year basis. You should also check your sales story and prepare revisions to strengthen it in places where your review shows such bolstering is needed.

After using the ideas described earlier in this chapter you may find it necessary to say, "I tried, and my management tried, but without success, to find a way to put through a five-year payment schedule for you. Fortunately, however, you can have our installation at $—— per month." In a fair percentage of such cases the prospect will sign the new order (with three-year payments) that you place before him at that point. His sales resistance is usually weaker than it was during your first call, and he may feel under some obligation to you.

When selling to the price shopper, decide whether you can sell quality. If you can't, then reduce the price to some denominator relative to use on a per day, per month, or per use basis.

KEY REVIEW POINTS FOR
SELF-IMPROVEMENT

Describe five steps in reducing the number of prospects who haggle over price or trade-in allowance.

What can you say when the price shopper won't let you give your sales presentation?

How do you shift the thinking of a price shopper to a quality emphasis?

How do you meet competition when your price is higher?

What sales strategies can you use to take the prospect out of the market?

Make price shoppers
quality buyers

Chapter 8

Outselling Competition

Know the **competition**
Improve on your own; **don't condemn** another
Win with your **approaches**—your **techniques**
The wherewithal to **succeed**
Inside story of Mr. Typical Salesman

THIS CHAPTER deals with proven methods of outselling competition. Mastering techniques of neutralizing competition gives you another means of increasing your sales effectiveness. Don't depend upon one or two selling gimmicks.

Know Your Competitors

There are many ways to minimize competition. The more you know about competitive products and competitors' sales literature and advertising, the more likely you are to have additional ideas along these lines. You can collect competitive literature at conventions, at showrooms, and sometimes from customers and salesmen. Study it, and plenty of ideas will develop for your own use.

When you approach a competitor's display to obtain literature, your best procedure is to tell him frankly who you are and what company you represent. Ask him if he minds giving you a piece of his literature. If you haven't tried this heretofore, you'll be gratified with the pleasant response you obtain. After all, wouldn't *you* courteously give *your* competitor a piece of literature if *he* openly asked for it?

If the prospect definitely intends to buy equipment of your type and you're able to eliminate *all* competition, you're almost sure to get the order. Just selling a prospect on your brand isn't always enough, because if you don't do a complete selling job he may make the purchase through his home office or through a friend or relative who sells the same brand.

Never Condemn Your Competitor

First of all, never condemn your competitor. Remember that "whatever they have is good." Be careful to explain to your prospect that you aren't attempting to "knock" any competitor. However, you will have to compare your product with the others, to let the prospect see how your engineers have tested and analyzed all the types of competitive products. Then explain your brand is *years ahead* of any other make in economy of operation and in cleanliness of operation and in dependability of operation. Further explain that, in making this comparison, you'll call all of the others "Whoosis," so that you'll not be in the position of "knocking" any competitor.

For instance, perhaps you're trying to sell a washing machine to Mrs. Sargent, and she says, "I like your machine very much, Mr. Salesman. However, one of my friends has a Whoosis washer, which she thinks is wonderful. I want to take a look at it before I make a definite decision."

Suppose you know from actual experience that the Whoosis is a much lighter machine than yours, that it is noisier, and that it vibrates. *Don't* say, "You'll be sorry if you buy that rattrap! It's so flimsy that it'll quickly shake itself to pieces. And its noise will deafen you."

Instead, try something like this: "Mrs. Sargent, when we designed this Fulton washer, our engineers made it a precision product, to keep vibration—which as you know produces wear and noise—at a minimum. The lighter a machine of this type is, the more noise it makes and the quicker it wears out, doesn't it? You can tell when I thump the tub that the Fulton is solidly constructed, can't you? Yet, heavy as it is, it's so easy to handle that you can push it with one finger. Here, try it! In spite of its sturdy construction, it's no trouble at all to move, is it? Actually, ours is the most solidly constructed washer on the market. I don't want you to believe my unsupported word when I say that, because I'm a salesman and in my enthusiasm I may exaggerate and mislead you. But here's a specification sheet for our washer, and one for that other one you mentioned. Look! According to their own printed figures, ours is over seventy-five pounds heavier than theirs, isn't it? You've been able to compare without leaving our showroom, haven't you? That insures less vibration and longer wear with our Fulton, and less noise too, doesn't it, Mrs. Sargent? Now you feel confident, not only of our modern features but also of the built-in sturdy quality, don't you? Just put your name right there, and you can have this wonderful new Fulton washer in your home tomorrow."

DON'T CONDEMN THE OLD; IMPROVE ON IT

If you're trying to persuade a prospect to change from another line of merchandise to your own brand, you'll get further ahead if you don't condemn the line that he owns or has carried for years.

You can try something like this: "You're not the kind of person, Mr. Walsh, to carry other than top-quality merchandise or to deal with other than a reputable manufacturer. I'm not here to tell you anything bad about the blankets you've been carrying or the people with whom you're doing business. Our company is a very fine concern to deal with and has a wonderful reputation. I'm sure that if you can see that both you and your customers would benefit by making a change, you would at least like to know what these benefits are so that you can come to a reasoned decision, wouldn't you?"

If you're trying to sell an idea, you'll find it wise not to condemn present conditions or policies. You can only hazard a chance at this when you have something better to offer. Even in such cases it's best to show the advantages of the new order, without condemning the old one too harshly.

If you say, "Your accounting system is cumbersome and old-fashioned," perhaps the man you say it to may have installed it. So you're calling him old-fashioned. He probably won't like this. Instead, you might try, "Would you be interested in a couple of improvements to your accounting system? It's quite possible that we could get the same results just as accurately and at lower cost."

When your prospect mentions a competitor's brand or you're attempting to let him see your points of superiority, don't ever *impress* the competitor's brand on the prospect's brain by repeating its name! Instead, you can call it "that other merchandise."

Selling Approaches to Beat Your Competitor

"YOU BE THE JUDGE" APPROACH

If you're making a comparison, you can say, "We don't want to condemn any competitor, Mr. Young. Yet, in all fairness to you, so that you can make a satisfactory choice, you should become familiar with our points of superiority. The only way I can let you see these points of superiority of our prime window is by comparison. We lump all our competitors together and call them 'Whoosis,' so we can give you a fair comparison and yet not knock any competitor. Here's a sample of our prime window, Mr. Young. Just these few screws to tighten, and it's in! Did any of the Whoosis windows have as low an installation cost as ours? That'll save you money, won't it? Look how air-tight it is! Were any of the Whoosis windows this tight? Look how sturdy it is, and how simple to operate! Were any of the Whoosis windows as sturdily and simply built as this? By keeping down service calls, that'll save you still more money, won't it? Although we have all these points of superiority, if I told you that our window costs no more than any of the Whoosis windows, would you give me the order right now?"

Where at all possible, the best policy is to talk your product and to tell the prospect, "*You* be the judge."

CASE EXAMPLE OF "YOU BE THE JUDGE" APPROACH

Frequently a customer will mention a competitor by name and ask, "What do you think of the Whoosis compressor?" Some salesmen answer by condemning the competitor violently: "It's terrible! The company that handles it is a bunch of crooks." Others damn it with faint praise: "For lightweight, cheaply constructed equipment, it's no worse than any of the other assembled compressors on the market. But of course it can't compare with ours in weight and sturdiness and precision engineering."

Both of the above answers are hazardous. When the prospect

demands, "What do you think of the Whoosis compressor?" a better reply is, "Mr. Allen, I'm not here to condemn any competitor—or even to talk about his product. My purpose is to let you see the points of superiority of my own compressor. Then *you* be the judge. *You* decide for yourself which one best suits your needs, which one you want."

AVOIDING THE "SECOND BEST" TRAP

People who consider themselves smart buyers frequently ask the salesman, "Granted that yours is the best equipment on the market, what brand do you consider second best?" Their reasoning is that if two or three salesmen of competing lines pick the same brand as second best, then it really is the best. Accordingly, that will be the best one to buy. If you're careless in answering this question, you may lose the order.

Therefore, when a prospect inquires what you consider the second-best equipment on the market, a good answer is something along the following lines: "Mr. Allen, they're all grouped together so far behind, I wouldn't know how to put them in any order of second, third, and so on. We have so many features of superiority that we're YEARS ahead of any other make. The other companies are grouped together several laps behind, trying hopelessly to catch up with us." Then show specifically wherein you are years ahead.

"YEARS AHEAD" APPROACH TO OUTSELL COMPETITORS

"Look! The television set is on. Here's our sales story:

"Sterling television sets are YEARS AHEAD of any other make in clearness of picture! Did you ever see a clearer picture, Mr. Rollins? Sterling television sets are also YEARS AHEAD in beauty of tone and fidelity of sound. Did you ever hear a lovelier and more natural receiver? Sterling television sets are YEARS AHEAD in simplicity of handling. Here's how your controls operate: on, off; louder, softer; brighter, duller; station change here— did you ever see anything simpler? Sterling television sets are YEARS AHEAD in beauty of styling. Aren't those lovely woods and beautiful lines?

"That's a powerful sales demonstration, isn't it, Mr. Rollins? Your salesmen can use it on their dealers, can't they? Remember, YEARS AHEAD of any other make in clearness of picture, sound fidelity, ease of handling, and beauty of design! Your dealers' salesmen can easily be trained in its use, can't they?"

THE PROFIT OR TURNOVER APPEAL

A manufacturer's salesman, demonstrating a television set to a potential wholesale distributor, may say, "Mr. Rollins, our line *is* slightly higher in price than some of the others in the field. Yet our distributors report outstanding volume and profits with it. The reasons are that: 1) we have a hard-hitting sales presentation; 2) this sales presentation is backed up by the operation of our television sets—the customer is the judge of any statements we make; 3) our sales presentation is short and easy for your salesmen to use on prospective dealers; and 4) it's easy for your salesmen to teach your dealers to use on their prospects to increase *their* sales volume—which, of course, means increased volume for *you*."

THE EXCLUSIVE-FEATURE APPROACH

Another way of weakening competition is by telling the story of the evolution of your industry and pointing out how many makes are struggling along without the modern features your product possesses. All of this, of course, should be done without mentioning the name of any competitor.

Example of a **sales story** to establish **exclusiveness** of your product and company:

To tell the story of the evolution of your product, suppose you're trying to sell a Blizzard combination electric refrigerator with low-temperature frozen-food compartments.

SALESMAN: "Mr. and Mrs. Edwards, did you know that the Blizzard Corporation is one of the oldest and most experienced companies in the refrigeration field?"

MR. EDWARDS: "Yes, I've heard of your firm for years."

SALESMAN: "Did you know that we were the first manufacturer to include the compressor as an integral part of the refrigerator? You probably don't remember that when electric refrigerators originally came upon the market, the mechanism and the refrigerator itself were separate and were frequently installed in two different locations, with the compressor often placed in the basement and the refrigerator on the first floor. Perhaps you *can* remember when ice cubes were hard to get out of the tray? Blizzard pioneered in easy-removal ice-cube trays. Then controlled cold was another development in which Blizzard was one of the leaders. More recently, you can remember, I'm sure, when automatic defrosting first became available? And now the newest development is zoned cold. This allows you to use part of your refrigerator for the storage of frozen foods while the remainder cares for items that shouldn't be frozen. Did you know that there are still refrigerators without automatic defrosters? You want the truly automatic refrigerator—one that works for you instead of your working for it, don't you?"

Selling Techniques to Beat Your Competitor

"DON'T BELIEVE ME—CHECK WITH OUR USERS"

Instead of helping your competitor, you can actually do many things that will tend to make his problem more difficult. From reading his literature or his newspaper or magazine advertisements, or from listening to and absorbing what various prospects tell you, you can often guess closely the steps that the lower-priced competitor will take to try to get the order away from you. If so, you can gauge part of your sales presentation accordingly.

For example, you can say something like this (in cases where you can't get the order otherwise): "Here's our complete users' list. You've heard the story of our product from me. Now, before you buy, perhaps you'd like to see what the actual user says about it. Notice that I'm handing you our *entire* list. You can choose the names and addresses you wish. Beware of the man who comes in with the hand-picked user list indicating where he wants to take you. Perhaps he'll offer to show you five or six of his nearby customers who appear to be satisfied. Why doesn't he let you choose, as we do, from his *complete* list? Is it because he's afraid you'll find some users who are unhappy? *We* don't do business that way. Here's our *entire* list —you do the picking *yourself!*"

EMPHASIZING EXCLUSIVE FEATURES

One of the many methods of eliminating competition is to emphasize your exclusive features. You might call it the "only with" method. Suppose your diesel motor has three exclusive features: rotomotor unit, sealed lubrication, and titanium injector. You explain and demonstrate the rotomotor unit. As you do, you emphasize the fact that it's exclusive: "This rotomotor unit is a unique feature developed by our engineering department. No other brand has it. This is the way it works. . . . This is what it does for you. . . ."

Then you try for three commitments: "Do you like our rotomotor unit? Have I made it clear how it will save you money? Don't you think that it's an excellent engineering advance?"

After the commitments, you ask, "Do you appreciate that *only with* our diesel motor you get the rotomotor unit?"

Use the same procedure with sealed lubrication and titanium injector. Then you summarize briefly: "Mr. Harrison, you've said that you like our exclusive features: our rotomotor unit, our sealed lubrication, and our titanium injector. I don't blame you for liking them, for they are marvelous pieces of engineering, and they're beautifully and sturdily constructed. *Only with* our product do you get the rotomotor unit, the sealed lubrication, and the titanium injector. Here!" (placing the order in front of him). "Put your name right there, and you'll get what you like and want."

THE "RATHER HAVE" APPEAL

Another method of eliminating competition is by using the "rather have" appeal. Examples follow:

"Wouldn't you *rather have* our brand, with its rotomotor unit, its sealed lubrication, and its titanium injector, than another brand without them?"

"Which would you *rather have*, our brand with its exclusive rotomotor unit, its patented sealed lubrication, and its unusual titanium injector, or some other make that doesn't provide these marvelous features?"

"Wouldn't you *rather have* the reliability, the convenience, and the saving in money that these exclusive features bring, than take a chance on another make that doesn't offer them?"

USING A CHART FOR YOUR PRODUCT

Sometimes a chart similar to that on page 97 is used to eliminate competition. If you can get the prospect to fill it in—

under your guidance—all the better. However, it isn't essential that he actually do the writing. So if he won't take the pencil in his hand readily, you yourself can make the necessary entries. The important thing is that they be made.

When filled in, this chart is an effective visual aid in eliminating competition. The superiority of your product stands out sharply. You should use it *to lead directly into the close.*

Previously, you've seen that you shouldn't mention a competitor's name, and some suggestions were given as to how to accomplish this. Instead of "Your Equipment," write the name of your product on the chart given below. Indicate your competitors by letters (X, Y, and Z) or by "Whoosis No. 1," "Whoosis No. 2," and "Whoosis No. 3." Tell your prospect

	YOUR EQUIPMENT	COMPETITOR X	COMPETITOR Y	COMPETITOR Z
Rotomotor Unit?	Yes	No	No	No
Sealed Lubrication?	Yes	No	No	?
Titanium Injector?	Yes	No	?	No
Strong Manufacturer?	Yes	Yes	No	?
Well-Established Distributor?	Yes	?	No	Yes
Adequate Service Organization?	Yes	?	?	Yes
Proved Economy?	Yes	?	?	?
Freedom from Service?	Yes	?	?	?

that you do this so that you won't be in the position of knocking any of them. Even if you're doing the writing—as you probably will be—ask him for the information that you fill in under the heading of each competitor. There'll probably be many more question marks than shown below, for he won't know the answers to many of the questions.

When it's all filled in—and the writing should be done plainly in front of the prospect, where he's sure to see it constantly—you can say something like this: "Mr. Foster, you appreciate the advantage of buying a diesel engine with a rotomotor unit, sealed lubrication, and a titanium injector, don't you? In addition, you want a strong manufacturer, a well-established distributor, an adequate service organization, proved economy, and freedom from service, don't you? Look at this chart! Our product gives you all of that. Don't you think you'd be wiser to buy our engine, where you're sure of getting these features, than any of these others, where you're doubtful about them?"

THE PROJECTIVE TECHNIQUE

Another way to eliminate competition is by projection. That is, you project the prospect's proposed choice of the competitive merchandise or service so that he can see the undesirable results of such choice. And you are careful to obtain commitments as to the undesirability of these results.

As an example of projection, let's listen in on a conversation between Ed Parker, president of a company manufacturing semiprepared food products such as cake mixes, and Bob Mitchell, the chief executive officer of one of his distributors.
PARKER: "Bob, when I got your letter the day before yesterday saying that you'd been approached by the Hanson people to take on their line, I wasn't surprised. As you know, Hanson is a new outfit and they're trying hard to get established. Frankly, Bob, you're the third of our distributors who's been approached. Both of the others turned them down flat, because of their long connection with us, their confidence in our merchandise, and the personal friendship that exists between us and our distributors, and because of the comfortable profit they have made from our franchise. I know that it was because of this same friendship, which I appreciate

and value highly, Bob, that you wrote me so frankly. Many, many thanks for your thoughtfulness and consideration. They are heart-warming. As soon as I read that section of your letter saying that you're going to take on the Hanson line instead of ours unless we can meet their lower price on one of their groups, I called our comptroller into my office and showed it to him.

"Naturally, being the head of our company, our monthly reports give me the detailed figures as to the costs and profits for each of our products. With the comptroller I went over, item by item, our last cost analysis statement, which had been prepared only a few days before. For if I can, not just because of the business involved but because of the long friendship we've had and because of the respect and affection I have for you, Bob, I want to do everything for you that I possibly can.—I hope you believe that."

MITCHELL: "I do, Ed."

PARKER: "Briefly, Bob, although we checked every figure most carefully, the simple arithmetic involved doesn't permit us to price our merchandise at any lower figure. If we did, we'd be operating that department at a loss, which is bad not only for us but for you and our other good customers. The same arithmetic applies to our competitors."

MITCHELL: "If that is so, Ed, how do you explain Hanson's lower price, which I confess is most appealing?"

PARKER: "Assuming that he's using the same high grade of raw materials that we are and is not lowering his quality below ours, and assuming that he has the same knowledge and long experience of the market that we have, he'd pay the same price for his basic materials that we do, wouldn't he?"

MITCHELL: "I guess he would."

PARKER: "You've seen the plants where we process our merchandise, and I remember your commenting that you didn't see how anyone could operate more efficiently. Do you recall saying that, Bob?"

MITCHELL: "Yes, and I still feel that way."

PARKER: "So he can't beat either the cost of our raw materials or our labor cost, can he?"

MITCHELL: "I guess not, Ed."

PARKER: "That leaves only his overhead and his profit to consider. We do such a terrific volume in our various departments that our overhead becomes a small fraction of our price to you. I know that the company you mention, which is just trying to get started, may not have quite as many employees on their staff as we have in our tightly knit organization. By the same token, with their physical plant considerably smaller than ours, their total plant operating dollar cost may be lower. However, because of their much smaller tonnage, the chances are ten to one that their *unit* overhead costs are higher than ours. Let's lean over backward, however, and say that their overhead costs per unit are the same. That leaves only profits to make up the rest of his price to you. The same arithmetic that applies to our figures applies to his. Two and two are four for us, but they're also four for him, aren't they, Bob?"

MITCHELL: "I guess they are."

PARKER: "Knowing how short is the profit margin on which we operate, and knowing that he's fortunate if his costs for the same quality are as low as ours, then I'd say that this salesman is using this one item as a 'come-on' loss leader to try to snag you as his distributor and to get you to take on his line instead of ours. Does that sound logical to you?"

MITCHELL: "Yes, it does, Ed. I feel the same way as you do. Yet business is business and money is money. Why shouldn't I take advantage of this opportunity to make more money, even if Hanson is running this one item at a loss?"

PARKER: "Let's answer you this way, Bob. If it's good business for you to do so, I agree with you that you should throw us out and take on this other company's line. And I believe you'll agree with me that if it isn't good business for you to handle his merchandise instead of ours, you should give him the old heave-ho. Right?"

MITCHELL: "Sure you're right, Ed; but how are we going to decide whether or not this *is* good business?"

PARKER: "Well, we're two individuals with plenty of experience and a reasonable amount of brains, so it shouldn't be too difficult for us to make a projection of what will probably happen if you listen to this chap's siren song and are motivated by it. From that projection you can easily determine whether it's better business for you to continue with our time-tested product and our friendly and mutually profitable relations, or to make this change into the unknown. The projection will take only a few minutes. Want to try it?"

MITCHELL: "Sure, why not?"

PARKER: "Right now, as I understand it, this potential competitor has no representation and no distribution in your area. Is that correct?"

MITCHELL: "Yes, that's right."

PARKER: "And we've agreed—and expressed it bluntly—that he's using the lure of a loss leader of one group of items to get you to establish his entire line in the large number of markets and stores and other outlets who are your customers. Right?"

MITCHELL: "Yes, that looks like what he's doing."

PARKER: "Do you remember, Bob, when you and I first worked together some eighteen years ago? It wasn't easy to get our products accepted by your customers at the start, was it?"

MITCHELL: "No, it wasn't."

PARKER: "We put in lots of hard licks together and spent considerable money advertising in newspapers and radio and later on television, didn't we?"

MITCHELL: "Yes, Ed, we did."

PARKER: "And we had some good promotional campaigns, too, so that today we have not only acceptance and good will by your customers for our brands, but also a steady volume from *their* satisfied retail customers. And our mutual connection gives us an acceptable profit, doesn't it?"

MITCHELL: "Yes, that's right."

PARKER: "Now let's consider the various things that will happen if you should take on the other line and throw ours out. First, although I feel most kindly toward you, Bob— and I hope we can continue our friendly and profitable relations for years to come—yet I can't permit a metropolitan center and trading area as large and prosperous as this to be a vacuum so far as our products are concerned. So I'd immediately take steps to obtain a new distributor. And because of the good will and volume and the profitable operation you and I have built up here, I don't believe that would be too difficult. Do you?"

101

MITCHELL: "I agree that it wouldn't be hard for you to find another distributor, Ed."

PARKER: "And this new distributor—at the beginning, anyway—would be cashing in on the effort and the money you and I have spent—on blood, sweat, and tears you've shed—in the past eighteen years, wouldn't he?"

MITCHELL: "Yes, he'd undoubtedly attempt to cash in on our prior investment."

PARKER: "We're loyal to you, Bob, and we've no intention whatsoever of severing our connection unless you force us to do so. Yours is an upstanding concern, of the caliber we like to do business with. You're an awfully nice guy yourself, and I've a deep personal affection for you. And, as I said before, our connection has been a mutually profitable one. By the same token, however, Bob, if our hypothetical new distributor merits it by measuring up to our high standards—and we'll make every effort to see that he does—then he'll receive from us that same deep loyalty that should now be your cherished possession. We wouldn't lightly take him on, nor lightly throw him out. So, no matter how great our friendship may be, Bob, and no matter how much you and I respect each other's characters and methods of operation, should you eliminate us and some time after taking on the other line find that it's a disappointment to you, we will *not*, as a matter of ethics and good business, discard our new distributor and take you on again. The only exception to this would be if he failed to measure up to our standards, which I consider most unlikely because of the care with which we choose our distributors."

MITCHELL: "What you're saying, Ed, is that if I'm once out, I stay out so far as you're concerned."

PARKER: "I didn't want to say it as bluntly as that, Bob, but you're exactly right! I hope you understand our position, and that you realize that there's nothing antagonistic or vindictive in our proposed action. We simply *must* insure the continuity and productivity of our business."

MITCHELL: "I understand that, Ed."

PARKER: "Just because this salesman comes to you and makes you an offer of one group of items at a money-losing price, Bob, I'm not going to reduce the price of my same items. As

I've said, the arithmetic of it doesn't permit me to take such drastic action. But if you take on his line of products—OR IF ANY OTHER DISTRIBUTOR IN THIS AREA DOES SO—and his merchandise gets into the retail stores and other outlets at a lower price than ours, we shall, after determining that it is the same high quality as ours, meet this competition by reducing our price. This will hurt us, and we shan't like it. But we believe it will hurt him more. First, because it pulls out from under him the all-important crutch on which he was leaning to secure your account, because then he'll be no lower in price than anyone else. Second, it deprives you of your strongest talking point in your attempt to introduce this unknown line of merchandise to the shelves of your customers' retail stores and markets, and to the supply houses of your other outlets, and finally to the pantries and kitchens of Mrs. Housewife. What argument have you got to persuade them to go from the known and satisfactory to the unknown and possibly unsatisfactory, except that of a lower price? And, when we take that away from you, your row becomes an awfully hard one to hoe, doesn't it?"

MITCHELL: "It could be."

PARKER: "The third reason why I believe this cut price will hurt this new salesman more than it does us is that he's new and hasn't established the profitable volume on his complete line of products that we have. As we agreed a few minutes ago, the same arithmetic that applies to us applies to him. Because of his smaller general volume, don't you think the discomfort from his loss leader will be more painful and more unbearable to him that it will be to us?"

MITCHELL: "It could be."

PARKER: "I believe that he'll holler 'Uncle!' and quit that foolishness long before we have any tendency in that direction. When his price on this one group of items goes back to its normal level, at that time, of course, we'll put ours back, too. Then where are you? If you've been unlucky enough to take on his merchandise, you'll be left struggling with a still relatively unknown line, and you'll be competing against our brands, which have been established here some eighteen years. Sure, our company will suffer, because he'll possibly get some volume that would have come to us. But won't you suffer more? Because you'll be left representing an outfit whose brands are relatively unknown; and do you think that in the few months' time that it would take all this to develop, you could build up a volume with this other brand as great as you and I have done in the past eighteen years?"

MITCHELL: "No, it doesn't seem likely, does it?"

PARKER: "No, Bob, it doesn't! So you'd be left representing an unknown line of merchandise, without real acceptance in this territory, against the competition of our established brand. Thus you'd have less volume and less profits than you now do, wouldn't you?"

MITCHELL: "It certainly seems that way, Ed."

PARKER: "Suppose at that time a miracle occurred and my new distributor failed to measure up to my requirements and I took you on again. You'd still be a loser, wouldn't you, Bob? Because you'd have less volume with our line than you now have. For of course you'd have developed some volume for this other chap. And a good share of his volume would be coming from our reduced total. So you and I would then have to work and strain and spend time and money to regain that volume. It would make you feel bad, wouldn't it, Bob, every morning during your shave to look in the mirror at your reflection and think regretfully, 'I'm sure sorry I did that to me!' Wouldn't it be better and more pleasant to think the opposite?"

MITCHELL: "I guess it would, Ed. Thanks a million for making everything so clear to me! Actually, I wanted to stay with you all along. I could sense that changing lines was the wrong thing to do, and this little conversation has simply crystallized and highlighted my unformed thoughts. I'd be a fool to make a change! . . . Come on, let's go have dinner."

Use **tact** with the projective technique:

A word of warning! If this projection method isn't handled with delicacy and tact, you can easily antagonize your prospect and lose all chance of getting the order. Be particularly sure not to condemn your competitor. Also, don't let anything you say be a criticism of your prospect's intelligence or judgment. Build him up in his own estimation. Get plenty of commitments as you go along. Be especially careful that none of your statements describing the projection sound like threats. Threats are a quick and nearly infallible way of antagonizing people.

Special Pointers for Competitive Salesmen

GET THE ORDER THEN AND THERE

Another way to eliminate competition is to get the order then and there. In a situation of this sort, be sure to close with plenty of commitments covering both your product and also the advantages of placing the order at that particular time. If you get the prospect's signature on the order, the only remaining danger is that a competitor may reach your customer and frantically attempt to upset your sale. The strength of your close is your best protection against this occurrence.

One thing that you must guard against is that the prospect may feel that you're applying pressure. Nobody likes to be high-pressured into buying. If you annoy the prospect, he'll dislike you and you'll lose the order.

OFFSETTING THE COMPETITIVE GUARANTY ADVANTAGE

If you know your competitor has a five-year guaranty whereas your product carries only a one-year guaranty, you can try something like this: "Here's our guaranty, Mr. Dutton. I'll read it to you, and then I'm going to hand it to you so that you can see I've given you every word of it, just as it's written. . . . Now that's clear and straightforward, isn't it? There are no hidden jokers in there, are there? You don't need to buy our oil, or our printing ink, or our plastic, or anything else from us for this guaranty to be effective, do you? That's real protection, isn't it? Our product must be good, or we couldn't make a guaranty like that, could we? The reason I'm stressing this guaranty, Mr. Dutton, is that some of the cheaper units that have no mechanical or engineering features comparable to ours have hit upon a so-called 'five-year guaranty' to snare unwary customers. If you should come across one of these products, don't just listen to what the salesman claims. Every sales contract contains a clause stating that no verbal statements are binding and that only what's printed in the contract will be followed. Therefore read carefully *every word* of these so-called 'five-year guaranties.' You'll find that they're hedged about with so many restrictive conditions that they may actually cost you money. For example, if you have to burn the distributor's oil in your heating equipment in order to obtain his so-called 'five-year guaranty,' did you know that a simple two-minute adjustment can make your burner use enough additional oil to more than make up for any so-called 'free service' that the salesman may promise you? So read *every* word and save yourself some headaches!"

DON'T MAKE IT EASY FOR YOUR COMPETITORS

One way of making it easy for competition is to suggest that the prospect look elsewhere. For example, beware of making a suggestion such as, "You can look all up and down automobile row and you will not find a car to equal this one" or, "Compare ours with the other two and you'll see for yourself that we're the biggest and best of the 'big three.' " We repeat, you're helping competition when you use suggestions such as those.

In countless other ways you can actually help your competitor take the order away from you. Watch out and guard against them.

For instance, suppose the prospect for a fork-lift truck asks, "Aren't there any other *good* makes of fork-lift trucks besides yours?"

Some salesmen answer, "Yes, I suppose there are."

This is an example of making it easy for competition. A better answer is something along these lines: "When you ask, 'Aren't there any other good makes besides yours?' Mr. Carter, it depends upon what you mean by that word 'good.' Some people might say, for example, that a man driving a Standard-bred horse and a rubber-tired ball-bearing buggy had *good* transportation. And at one time there was none better. But honestly, if you're going to buy transportation for yourself and your family today, you'd choose a current-model automobile over this fine horse and buggy, wouldn't you, Mr. Carter? Well, we're as far ahead of competition as the current-model automobile is of the horse and buggy—no matter how fine a horse or how good a buggy you could get. So when you ask me if there aren't other *good* makes of fork-lift trucks besides

106

mine, I can only reply with another question. Do you want the features that make trucks *good* today, or do you want the features that were called *good* (like the horse and buggy) years ago?"

Another way you can help competition is by failing to explain or demonstrate the superior points of your equipment. If you don't tell a good story (which is covered in Chapter 3), you'll help competition.

If you quote your price without making sure that the prospect knows *why* your product is giving him more for his money, you're making it easy for price-cutting competition to take the order from you.

DEVELOP A SALES STORY TO OUTSELL THE THE PRICE-CUTTER

Don't say, "Mr. Jensen, the price of this sofa is $350"—and stop there. Instead, continue, "While you know and I know that you can purchase others at lower figures, you're getting more than a good buy at this price. That's because the beautiful mahogany is solid—not a veneer. Also, the lovely upholstery fabric is of the finest quality that money will buy, and it's been mothproofed. It's smooth and pleasant to the touch, isn't it? It feels comfortable when you sit on it, doesn't it? That's because the inner springing and the webbing and the filling materials are of dependable quality. Thus today's comfort and beauty will last as long as you own it. Its quality and beauty and built-in comfort make it a good buy, don't they, Mr. Jensen?"

COMPETING WITH FLASHY SALES PROMOTION

Sometimes a prospect is attracted by competitive literature that appears to be more impressive than yours. If you find such a situation, you can try something along this line: "Don't be taken in by flashy literature, Mr. Grant! Doesn't it cost much less for a company to pay ten cents extra for a flashy, impressive piece of literature than for it to add the fine engineering and the skilled labor and the genuine material that make a quality product? Often the sleaziest merchandise has the most impressive literature, doesn't it? Did you ever see the kind of paper the nonexistent gold mines in Canada use to sell blue-sky stock to gullible Americans? After all, it isn't what's written in the literature that protects you, but what's in your sales contract, isn't it? Aren't you lots wiser, Mr. Grant, if, instead of buying on the basis of extravagant claims in glowing literature, you buy on the basis of the quality of the products and the standing and integrity of the company who makes it?"

BEATING YOUR COMPETITION TO THE PUNCH

On many sales, you know the type of story your competitors will tell the prospect. In fact, to be a salesman worthy of the name, you should be familiar with the selling points of your principal competitors. When you're in this position, you can frequently steal their thunder and beat them to the punch by utilizing their claims in your own story.

For example, suppose you're selling an oil burner that is made entirely by one manufacturer. And suppose you know that competitors selling assembled burners say, "If you buy our equipment, should you ever need a new motor or fan or pump or controls, any standard brand will fit our unit. You aren't required to buy one manufacturer's product and pay a high price for it. You can buy where you can get the best service, and the best price."

Knowing this, when you describe your burner you can say, "Which would you rather have, Mr. Hill—a burner whose parts are made in one factory, each part for the others, thus ensuring long life and quietness and economy, or a burner whose parts may come from five or six different factories, depending upon who can make them lightest and cheapest and sell them for the least? Since our motor, fan, and pump are all made in one plant, each part for the others, there's no vibration. We don't muffle misfits with cradled spring mountings or trick couplings because we don't need to. We think there's little likelihood that you'll ever need to replace one of these elements. Yet we try to protect you, Mr. Hill. Should such an occasion arise, we have looked out for your interests. You aren't required to install *only* our replacement motor or *only* our fan or *only* our pump. Instead, we've built our burner so that, if you should so desire, you can use any standard brand for replacement. But we don't believe that you'll ever need to do so in the next twenty years."

If you know that your competitors are featuring a five-year guaranty vs. your one-year guaranty, you may find it advantageous to bring up the subject without waiting for either a competitor or the prospect to mention it.

You would introduce the subject of a guaranty by saying something like this: "You've seen our guaranty and the protection it affords you, Mr. Ivey." Then you go on from there with your sales story.

What Makes Mr. Typical Salesman Tick?

Don K. Johnson, an outside salesman for John J. Garrett Co., Inc., of Anderson, Indiana, was selected as the nation's Typical Jobber Salesman. He is described this way:

"A talk with several of Mr. Johnson's customers revealed he is well liked, gives good service, is prompt and never promises something he can't deliver.

"Bill Rees, parts manager for the Crown City Chevrolet Co., in Albany, Ind., put it this way:

" 'Don is dependable. He won't give you a 'snow-job' just to sell something. He calls with regularity and he's hell-bent on service. What more could a guy ask.' "

Mr. Johnson regards himself as having a conservative selling approach and follows these six points with gusto:

"1. Above all, give a customer the best service available.

2. Sell yourself to your customer.

3. Know the limitations of your customer.

4. Know the product you sell.

5. Make a complete check of stock. This is important because, should a customer fail to find an item he needs, he may lose confidence in the salesman.

6. Be of help to a customer. Never brush off his smallest request."*

KEY REVIEW POINTS FOR SELF-IMPROVEMENT

Should you condemn a prospect's present line of merchandise?

Why not?

* *Jobber Topics,* March, 1958, pp. 71-81, 112.

Why shouldn't you mention competitive brands by name? How can you avoid doing this?

When a prospect asks you what you think of specific competitive equipment, what should you answer?

What's a good reply when a prospect asks, "What brand do you consider second best?"

How can you construct your sales story to emphasize clearly your brand's points of superiority without mentioning any other makes?

What is the advantage of telling the story of the evolution of your product?

Name three ways in which you can make it easy for competition.

Can you think of several ways in which you can make it difficult for competition?

How can you use the same techniques used for outselling competition to get a raise or promotion for yourself?

Build up your own product or service
to overcome competition

Chapter 9

Seventeen Tips for Stepping up Your Selling Effectiveness

Emphasize the **positive**
Make a distressing idea **desirable**
Magnify savings and advantages
Tell the **bad news** first
Maintain your planned sales story
Use your **sales aids**
Sell husband and wife **together**
Use **sales clinchers** at the right time
Use the **telephone** wisely
Be **respected,** not rushed
Be **enthusiastic,** not excitable
Don't stay **overtime**
Let the buyer **know** you **want** the order

YOUR MASTERY and application of the seventeen tested selling strategies in this chapter will really step up your effectiveness.

TIP 1: EMPHASIZE THE POSITIVE

The expert salesman emphasizes the positive and eliminates the negative. He follows this principle in his personal attitude toward his product, his employers, and his work. The same idea applies also to his—and your—sales presentation.

You'll sometimes see so-called salesmen—and they usually don't last long in their jobs—who are constant gripers. The product they're trying to sell (?) is "terrible." Their employer is a "first-class jerk." Selling is "awful." If they could get a "real job," they "wouldn't be selling." Such men are negative-minded. The probabilities are that they would react in a similar manner to any other type of work to which they might change.

There's no perfect product, no perfect company, and no perfect individual. If you let the small imperfections of your product, your company, or your boss overshadow their good attributes and desirable features, you'll be unhappy as well as unsuccessful. Remember, there are many concealed bare spots, and many brown spots too, in that pasture on the other side of the fence that now looks so much greener than your own field! You won't see these defects until you've made the fatal jump. And then it may be too late to reconsider.

To say it slightly differently, *you're not the only one* who has problems. Your competitors have some too.

When making a sales presentation it is, of course, elementary to guard against such statements as, "You wouldn't want to buy any more insurance, would you?"

That's one type of negativism that should be avoided. Another type, more subtle perhaps, but strongly defeatist, comes from the prospect himself. If you accept these negative ideas from him, then your sales story becomes negative.

Let's suppose that you're a real estate salesman, and you're trying to sell an old-fashioned suburban home that has no garage. Your prospect and his wife have specified to you that they *must* have a garage in which to keep their car. When they see the house, it meets all their requirements except this one.

The wife is annoyed. She says, "We told you plainly that we must have a garage! You're just wasting our time by showing us this house without one!"

NEGATIVE SELLING

If you handle this negatively, you tell the prospect that you're sorry, but this house was so well built and on such a pleasant street that you just couldn't resist showing it to them. As for a garage, you mention the fact that they can probably rent one from a neighbor. This negative attitude on your part puts you on the defensive. If you continue in this manner, you're sure to lose the sale.

POSITIVE SELLING

If, on the other hand, you handle it positively, you say, "I showed you this house deliberately, with all your requirements in mind. Look over there! Your garage will go in that space

112

next to the beautiful oak tree, without harming it in the least. You'll still be left with sufficient room for a garden and for recreation. The driveway can run along this side of the house. The cost can be included in the financing of your home. I've allotted a big enough space so that you can have a double garage. One side of it can be rented to a neighbor, and you can use the income either to reduce your monthly mortgage payments or for other purposes, just as you wish. Even with the small additional cost of the garage, this property is a wonderful buy. And when all your payments have been cleared up some years from now, the income from the garage can help you pay your taxes every year thereafter."

As another example of emphasizing the positive and eliminating the negative, consider two salesmen who are being fed prospects by their managers or suppliers from a telephone canvass and direct-mail inquiries. Admittedly, these "prospects" may be weak. They may be hardly more than high-grade "suspects." Perhaps all that has actually been done by the telephone canvassers or by a direct-mail piece is to let the "prospect" know that something is available.

NEGATIVE SELLING

The negative-minded salesman spends time and effort in proving that "the prospect is no good. That's just a *name* you gave me! Those folks aren't interested in our product. I called them on the telephone to find out, and they told me not to come to see them." Naturally, he doesn't make many sales from this source.

POSITIVE SELLING

The positive-minded salesman receives the same type of name from the same source. He quickly realizes that these names are high-grade "suspects" and governs himself accordingly. His efforts are directed toward completing the work begun by the telephone canvasser or through direct-mail efforts, and in a *personal* face-to-face call he attempts to convert such people into actual prospects. As a result, he obtains a good volume of sales from the same type of name the negative-minded salesman has labeled "no good."

Illustrative sales interview with a **positive touch:**

A sales conversation at the door might run along the following lines:

SALESMAN: "Mrs. Harris, I'm not here to talk to you *now*. I just wonder when you can spare two minutes to answer a question."

MRS. HARRIS: "I guess I can spare two minutes right now, if that's all you want."

SALESMAN: "I'm Mr. Parker of the Sturgis Company. The young lady in our office suggested that I call and see if you and Mr. Harris might like to save money on your heating bill and might like to have a more comfortable home, both in summer and winter. So my question is: Would tonight, or tomorrow night, when Mr. Harris is home, be a better time for me to return and take a few measurements and give you an estimate on giving you greater economy, more comfort, and increased health by protecting your home with our blown-in- rock-wool insulation?"

In idea-selling—such activities, for example, as asking for a raise—it's important to emphasize the positive and eliminate the negative. Mention clearly and specifically your various accomplishments that have benefited your company. Don't bring up things that you might have done or didn't do because of various excuses. It's important to guard against introducing disagreeable or displeasing ideas. "No negative selling" applies here with as much force as it does in the sale of merchandise or of intangibles.

You're reminded elsewhere in this book that the productive salesman keeps on a "you" basis—that is, he presents the problem from the prospect's point of view. However, don't say in your try for either employment or a promotion, "Mr. West, I know you're trying to hold down expenses and not to add to our fixed overhead." Instead, try something like this: "Mr. West, I know you want to strengthen your organization by adding men of proved ability"; or, "Mr. West, I know you always make it a point to reward achievement."

When we say "No negative selling," we're not talking merely about the old and obviously wrong sample, "You wouldn't want to buy a vacuum cleaner today, would you, lady?"

Keep in mind the selling features of your product that, if

not carefully handled, may put negative or unpleasant thoughts in the prospect's mind. Here is an example from home-freezer selling: "The trays slide readily and are easily removed, so that *when you have to scrape off the ice* during defrosting *you won't need to work so hard.*"

TIP 2: SUBLIMATE A DISTRESSING IDEA

If a distressing idea simply must be touched upon, it is wise to refine it and change it into something desirable. Perhaps the whole idea can't be changed, but careful search may bring out beneficial aspects that you can stress.

The insurance salesman, for example, usually either skirts or entirely eliminates the idea of death—and even the word "death"—from his sales presentation.

He rarely says, "Mr. Randall, everyone who has ever been born has died or will die. Therefore you know you're going to die. Upon your death, how will your family be supported?"

Instead, his presentation runs along these lines: "Mr. Randall, wouldn't you like to provide for your son's college education? And wouldn't you like to retire while you and your wife are young enough to do things and enjoy activities that appeal to you?"

TIP 3: MAGNIFY SAVINGS AND ADVANTAGES

The expert salesman magnifies savings and advantages and shrinks expenses and costs. You've seen that you should always tell the truth when you sell. When you magnify the savings or shrink the expenses, therefore, this doesn't mean that you should exaggerate or alter the truth or tell lies. It does mean, rather, that you should put your best foot forward.

Sales interview illustrating how to **magnify savings:**

Suppose, for example, you're trying to sell an automobile manufacturer a stamping machine that will save him fifty cents on each of 300,000 cars he produces each year. If you talk to him about "fifty cents per car," your selling isn't nearly as strong as if you talk to him about "$150,000 per year of additional profits." You've legitimately magnified the savings from fifty cents to $150,000. That's SOME magnification.

Shrinking the cost is just the opposite. If your machine costs

115

$60,000, you don't keep reminding your prospect of this sizable outlay. Instead, you shrink it by making it clear that, based on the 300,000-per-year production, the cost is only twenty cents per car for the first year. After that the cost is nothing. On a ten-year basis—the estimated life of the machine—the cost is only two cents per car. However, the saving is fifty cents per car, so that the net gain is forty-eight cents per car over the next ten years.

Or, looking at it for the ten-year period in total, a $60,000 outlay will save $150,000 the first year. So in the first twelve months the manufacturer will get back his cost plus $90,000 or 150 per cent return on his money. And in the next nine years he'll get back, in addition, nine times $150,000, or $1,350,000, which gives a total net return of $1,440,000 after paying back his small initial investment of $60,000. How can he turn you down?

If you're selling a product whose saving over a lower-priced competitor is small—say $20 a year—you can magnify it by talking of the savings in terms of the life of your equipment.

For example: "Would you be interested in saving $400, Mr. Sawyer? Because of our boiler's exclusive features, we save you $20 a year, which is $400 savings during its life of twenty years. You've told me that I'm $150 high. But don't you see that actually I'm $250 low in over-all cost? Don't you think that investing $150 to make $400 is worth your while?"

Another way of legitimately magnifying savings and shrinking expenses is by discussing the problem in terms of capital investment. Suppose, for example, your product will save $50 a year.

To magnify it you say, "Mr. Clement, maybe $50 a year looks small to you; but let's consider it for a moment from the capital-investment point of view. You probably own some government bonds. Most of us do. They're the safest investment we can own. Their yield has been 2½ per cent, which is $25 per year for each $1000 bond. Thus the saving of $50 per year provided by my freezer is equivalent to the income on $2000 of government bonds. If I should hand you, as a gift, $2000 of government bonds, you'd be pleasantly surprised, wouldn't you? You wouldn't turn them down, would you? When you purchase my commercial freezer, Mr. Clement,

116

from an income point of view the savings produce the same equivalent as if I actually presented to you $2000 of government bonds. The freezer costs only $1500. So from an income or capital-investment point of view, you're $500 better off after buying my equipment. That's worth while, isn't it?"

If your equipment is $100 higher than competition and you want to shrink the difference, you can explain to the prospect that, from a capital-investment–government-bond point of view, he's giving up only $25 a year of income to own your product. The savings each year are much greater than that, so from an income point of view he's far ahead, and the $25 a year should prove no deterrent.

ADDITIONAL TECHNIQUES FOR MAGNIFYING SAVINGS

There are other methods of shrinking expenses or costs and of magnifying savings. As an instance of this, railroads have purchased more and more diesel locomotives to replace their coal-burning steam locomotives. The railroad managements know that the financial aspect of the transaction is highly advantageous to them. Details are given below, therefore, not so much to help the diesel locomotive salesman close the order as to give you a clue that may be of help in selling your own merchandise.

Suppose that the railroad considered purchasing $2,000,000 worth of diesel locomotives, and that the management knew this investment would save $200,000 per year (after allowing for maintenance and depreciation) over their operation of steam locomotives. The railroad would borrow $2,000,000 on twenty-year equipment trust notes at 3.5 per cent interest. It would further provide an annual 5 per cent sinking fund to retire the notes on an annual basis. Since the reduction of the notes provides a constantly decreasing interest payment, the average interest cost would be approximately one-half of 3.5 per cent, or 1.75 per cent per year. The 5 per cent sinking fund, plus 1.75 per cent interest, would give an annual finance charge of 6.75 per cent, or $135,000, to be deducted from the $200,000 per year saving. This would leave a net annual saving (while paying the debt in full) of $65,000. In twenty years the railroad would gain $1,300,000 by buying the $2,000,000 worth of diesel locomotives (in addition to retiring the debt incurred for their purchase).

TIP 4: TELL THE BAD NEWS FIRST

Expert salesmen tell the bad news first. Suppose your "bad news" is that your product is the highest priced on the market, and that, in addition, you can't make delivery for twelve months. Which is better, to bring out the bad news at the very beginning or to delay it until the end?

Remember the thermal gradient of a sale described in Chapter 1. Recall that you, the salesman, are trying to take your prospect, who may be freezing or at best only barely warm, up to the boiling point. So you give him a masterful sales presentation. You get him up to a closing temperature. The order is on the desk for signature, and the bad news of the high price and the twelve-month delivery are then presented. You couldn't reduce his buying temperature more quickly in any manner! While he's at a low buying temperature, how are you going to regain his interest?

You've used your best selling points. When you rehash these same points, they've lost some of their effectiveness. It's three or four times as difficult to get him into a buying mood the second time as it was originally.

Why not enhance his buying interest and keep him there? Doesn't that sound sensible? It can be done by giving him the bad news *before* you give him your major selling points. Then, once in a buying mood, you won't have anything to tell him that might reduce his buying interest. He'll remain at the boiling point, and you can move in to the close.

A sales interview on how to tell the bad news first:

An illustration is the case of the salesman of the highest-priced automatic heating unit on the market. His production was low and he was dissatisfied. In talking to his sales manager he said, "I get them all excited about our unit. But when I tell them the price, preparatory to signing them up, they lose all interest. What's wrong?"

The sales manager persuaded him to quote the price of the unit at the very beginning of the sales presentation. He coached the salesman so that he didn't say, "Our unit is priced at $1500. It's the highest-priced in the field."

Instead, he advised the salesman to say something like this: "At the very beginning, I want to let you know that the price of our automatic heating unit is $1500, the monthly payments coming to $43 a month if your down payment is $200. You know and I know that you can buy other units for less money, with monthly payments two or three or four dollars less per month. But in just a minute or two you're going to see why this unit is the *lowest-cost* unit that you can buy."

The salesman was further instructed that at this point he should plunge into his sales presentation.

The results were highly satisfactory. The salesman became a high producer and a high earner, simply by making this one change in his sales technique. He told his bad news first instead of at the end of his sales presentation, as he had done.

TIP 5: NEVER DISCARD YOUR PLANNED SALES STORY

When you concentrate your selling statements on a key objection, that doesn't mean you should discard your established, hard-hitting sales story. Far from it! What you should do is to tell your standard story. As you develop each of your major points, focus and aim them so that they strike hard on the key objection.

If we continue to use as our example the man who said, "I can't afford it; I haven't the money," after determining that he actually has *some* money you should proceed with the sale. If his objection of "no money" has been given at the beginning of the sales interview, you can use the method that follows as you give your sales story. If his objection has been given at the end of your presentation, you can utilize the same plan, incorporating it in a *strong summary*.

Demonstrate and explain your first major point. As you do this, adapt and mold your presentation so as to emphasize the fact that the prospect *can* afford your product. Get commitments, then proceed to the succeeding points, which you handle in the same manner.

Assuming that your product is air conditioning and that five of your major points are comfort, health, increased productivity, sealed unit, and patented ultra-compressor, you can focus each of these points on *economy*.

Talking of comfort, you might say, "Mr. Seward, you know it isn't the heat that gets you down so much as it's the humidity.

Our unit squeezes the moisture right out of the air. As soon as you come into the room, you feel relief. Have you ever noticed that tempers are shorter when people are hot and uncomfortable? Can you make the best decision when you're uncomfortable and irritable? Can this installation save you lots more than the small sum it costs?"

When you speak of health, it's easy to mention the amount of doctors' bills saved by air conditioning. Increased productivity is another feature that is readily focused on the money-saving, money-making goal. The higher the productivity, the more profitable will be the investment. The sealed unit can be aimed against the price target by pointing out the freedom from service and the economy that it effects. The ultra-compressor, with greater capacity, uses less electricity and also saves money.

Above all, don't drop your regular story and concentrate solely on price. Sure, you're going to mention the monthly payments and how small they are, and the savings that your equipment will bring. But while you're doing this you're going to be telling your regular, planned, hard-hitting story.

TIP 6: USE YOUR SALES AIDS PROPERLY

The expert salesman has his order pad out from the very beginning. Usually a sales presentation is made with the help of a sales album, or photographs, or charts, or booklets, or a sample demonstrator, or a combination of these items.

Demonstrating the product or service effectively can do three things that are important for every salesman:
1. Get and hold attention
2. Prove a selling point
3. Appeal to the emotions.*

When you're producing these accessories from your brief case BEFORE starting your presentation, it's wise to get out the order pad and have it lying plainly on the table or desk in front of your prospect. Let him become accustomed to seeing it before and during your demonstration. Then he won't be too shy when you put it into his hands at the close. Moreover, you'll save a possibly awkward pause should you have to fish

* Zenn Kaufman, "Cracking the Hard Ones with Showmanship," *The American Salesman,* January, 1958, pp. 29–36.

in your brief case to search hurriedly for an elusive order pad *after* you've brought the prospect up to the boiling point.

Expert salesmen make it easy for a prospect to buy and hard not to do so. If you're handing the order and the pen to the prospect for a signature, be sure that there's ink in the pen and that it will write. Have a desk or table or other firm surface on which he may write. Make a big black "X" on the order at the point of signature—the bigger and blacker it is, the more effective it will be.

Be sure to have the order form out in the open and at a convenient location, so that there is no awkwardness or delay when you reach for it.

When, as, and if you're able to place the order and the pen in the prospect's hands, it's not always too easy for him to divest himself of them. However, you must guard against the possibility of your losing physical control of these two sales tools. He may hold them and do nothing with them.

Expert salesmen use their sales equipment—with discretion. If you work for a company that supplies you with a sales album and perhaps a demonstration model, be sure to use them. Sometimes there may be a hundred or more pages of pictures, diagrams, charts, tables, etc. in the sales album. You're *not* obligated to make the prospect look at every one of these hundred pages. In trying to do so, you can talk yourself out of the order.

However, you should familiarize yourself with the sales helps that have been provided and utilize those portions of them that assist you in dramatizing and strengthening your sales presentation. Perhaps you can discover other vivid and impressive devices to enhance your story. Remember that if you spend your time in talking, without letting the prospect see any pictures or handle your demonstrator, you're trying to make your sales impression on only one of his five senses. The more of his five senses (hearing, seeing, feeling, smelling, and tasting) your story appeals to, the more powerful will be its effects.

Expert salesmen use paper and pencil. Be sure to include in your sales kit a pad of paper on which you can make sketches, do figuring, and write essential points during your sales presentation. You should take this pad out of your brief case before you start your selling story and have it convenient for use at any time during the interview.

If you have a well-organized sales-presentation album, whereby you conduct your prospect from page to page of descriptive pictures, sketches, and diagrams, you may not have much need for your pencil and paper. Even here, however, successful salesmen have found it helpful to jot down their key selling points in outline form on the pad as they go through the sales album.

Suppose, for example, the first four pages of your album contain pictures, diagrams, etc., portraying the convenience of your product. You'd say something like this: "The first advantage, Mr. Van Dyke, that our product brings you is convenience."

Here you write legibly (or print) on the pad the word "convenience." Have the pad plainly visible to the prospect, so that the key words that you write on it strike his eyes constantly. Continue with the pages of your sales album, giving your regular sales story. However, as you come to each key point, you write it boldly and legibly on your pad in turn.

Expert salesmen use visuals in summarizing and closing. You can say something like this: "Look at all these advantages that our product brings: 1. Convenience; 2. Comfort; 3. Cleanliness. Have I made it clear that these advantages mean money saved for you? Don't you feel that this is a good investment? Don't you believe that these benefits will build greater productivity and expand good will among your employees?"

Expert salesmen appeal, when possible, to all five senses. Psychologists tell us we obtain stronger impressions when an appeal is made to all of them. When the prospect listens to you talk, he's obtaining his knowledge of your product only through the one sense of hearing. If you add a pencil and paper to your sales kit, and use them, you strengthen your sales presentation by adding the customer's sense of sight as an absorptive mechanism working for you, or by supplying an additional medium for the use of this sense.

TIP 7: SAVE TIME AND SELL HUSBAND AND WIFE TOGETHER

If at all possible, expert salesmen sell husband and wife together, particularly if the signatures of both are required on the order. Naturally this statement doesn't apply to the diesel locomotive salesman or to sales made to businesses. It's slanted to the salesman of home equipment or home improvements. For such items, you'll usually find it advisable to sell husband and wife together.

Sometimes the husband says, "Come on in, Mr. Salesman, and tell me all about your product. My wife isn't home, but I can pass the information on to her, and she does just what I say anyway."

In such a case you can ask, "Do you mean to say that you'd give me the order tonight, without consulting her?"

If he hedges on the answer you can say, "I think you're right, Mr. Warren. I always talk over such purchases with *my* wife. After all, this item is for the home, which our wives run. They should certainly be consulted. While it's true that you can pass on to her anything that I tell you, I've found that the women frequently have questions—and very good ones— about subjects connected with our product that we may not have covered in our sales story. I've another call to make. How would tomorrow evening do, at about this same time?"

Sometimes there can be no escape from giving your sales presentation to only one half of the husband-wife team. In such a situation you'll find it helpful to use your paper and pencil carefully, so that you can leave a simple, legible outline of your sales story, to be used by your substitute. You won't burden this substitute with masses of literature, but one or two pieces with explanatory pictures will be helpful.

TIP 8: USE SALES CLINCHERS AT THE RIGHT TIME

During some sales presentations you'll have a "sales clincher" to help you. Expert salesmen don't use such clinchers until the order can be obtained. *A sales clincher is a special offer, or a condition, or an arrangement, that should have overwhelming weight in making a close.* The sales clincher should not be used until the order actually can be signed, then and there.

Suppose, for example, that the prospect has said that if you'll include a dual-limit control with the installation he'll give you the order. In trying to obtain acceptance of this condition you telephone your headquarters from the prospect's office, but your sales manager and your chief engineer are out of town.

What you can do here is to take a chance and write up the order, including in it: "This order is contingent upon our furnishing and installing a dual-limit control in addition to the standard equipment specified herein, and is to be canceled in case we are unable to furnish and install said dual-limit control." Then you should get the prospect to sign, and thus you take him out of circulation while you're determining if you can supply him with the extra that he requests.

Suppose, however, you walk out of his office without getting him to sign. A day later your engineering department informs you that the dual-limit control your prospect requested is approved. If you need his name on the dotted line, *do not go to the telephone and call him to tell him the good news. You can't get that signature over the telephone.* Instead, give him the good news in a personal call, when you can put the order in front of him for signature. Even where a verbal commitment is acceptable, personal contact is stronger than letter or telephone, although each year hundreds of millions of dollars of business are done through use of the latter medium. When you make the follow-up call, be sure to get a commitment so that the prospect will give you the order, before you use a sales clincher.

Sales interviews illustrating the use of **sales clinchers:**

SALESMAN: "Mr. Carlson, when I saw you on Wednesday, it's my recollection that you were favorably impressed with our shaper—with its over-all design, the quality of its workmanship, the reputation of its manufacturer, and the standing of our company who distributes it. The price, too, was satisfactory, as I recall it. In fact, the only thing that stood between you and me and the order was the feed. Is that right?"

MR. CARLSON: "Yes."

SALESMAN: "My recollection is that if I could deliver you this shaper with left-hand feed, instead of right-hand feed, on the same date and at the same price as you have on my literature there, you'd give me the order right now. Is that correct?"

Another example of the use of sales clinchers can be taken from the home-appliance field, where the signatures of both husband and wife are usually required on the order. If a specified condition for signing the order has been advanced by either of them on a previous visit and you're able to meet that condition on a return call, don't use your sales clincher unless both are present. Instead, make another appointment for a time when both signers will be available. You can tell the one on hand that you're working on the problem and that you hope to have the final word on your next call.

Salesmen must be constantly alert for opportunities to create new sales clinchers. Remember that a sales clincher is a special offer, or a condition, or an arrangement, that might have overwhelming weight in making a close.

Suppose, for example, you're selling home freezers. After your sales demonstration Mr. and Mrs. Foster, the prospects, seem to like and to want your freezer. Mr. Foster says, "I won't have the money for the down payment until pay day—the fifteenth of the month."

Don't reply, "If you sign the order now and give me a dollar, I can reserve your freezer. I'll return on the fifteenth for the balance of the down payment."

Instead, turn your reply into a committing question. Be sure to phrase it strongly enough to make a clincher out of it, something like this: "If I could take only one dollar from you tonight and come back on the fifteenth for the balance of the down payment, would you give me the order right now?"

The subject of the prospect's question or remark may be such a prosaic thing as: the location of an air conditioner; a certain color combination on a new car; delivery date sooner than normal; installation of heating equipment in winter without chilling the house; or delivery and installation now, with the first monthly payment due next fall (fall dating).

To all of these, the professional salesman doesn't say, "Oh, I can do that for you!"

Instead, he waits to give a definite answer until he's proceeded sufficiently far with his sales demonstration to secure enough commitments to justify a close. At the same time he may even deliberately build up the difficulty in the prospect's mind by a reply along these lines: "You've given me a tough assignment to solve that problem. I was intending to handle the subject shortly, Mr. Harding. Do you mind if I make a note of it, so that I don't forget it, and try to cover it in a few minutes?"

Then later, when he feels that the number of commitments he's obtained from his sales presentation justifies the question, he presents his clincher:

NOT: "Yes, we can put the air conditioner behind that partition,"

BUT INSTEAD: "If we put the air conditioner behind that partition, will you give me the order right now?"

NOT: "Yes, we can give you that blue-and-gray color combination, just like your sister's car,"

BUT INSTEAD: "If we can deliver that blue-and-gray color combination, just like your sister's car, will you put your name on this order right now?"

NOT: "Yes, we can have that piano delivered tomorrow,"

BUT INSTEAD: "If we can make delivery tomorrow, are you ready to buy right now?"

NOT: "Yes, we can install this wonderful new furnace, using our winter schedule so that you don't suffer from lack of heat,"

BUT INSTEAD: "If we can install this wonderful new furnace, using our winter schedule so that your house temperature won't drop enough to make you uncomfortable, are you ready to close this deal right now?"

NOT: "Yes, we can install this automatic heating unit now, with the first monthly payment due next fall,"

BUT INSTEAD: "If we can install this money-saving automatic heating unit now, so that you can obtain the benefits of even, economical heat without effort on your part during the changeable days of spring and late summer, and yet you won't need to start paying for it until next fall, will you go ahead with this transaction right now?"

Remember, when you've used questions such as those above, you've made no promise and no actual reply to the prospect's question. Instead, you've been trying for the big commitment from him. Therefore if the prospect answers to your clincher, "No, I'm not ready to sign up yet," you can say:

"There must be something else that is holding up the order,

in addition to this problem we're trying to solve. If you'd be willing to tell me what is the second problem, I'll try to help you solve it while I'm working on the first one."

Here the prospect may give you another obstacle that you can convert into an additional clincher, so that you have two clinchers to confront him with instead of one.

Before using these two clinchers, however, it may be well to obtain further commitments, either by proceeding with your planned sales presentation or by giving a summary of the portions you've already covered. In this way you can make sure that your prospect is near the boiling point.

If it's getting late at this point, so that you or the prospect must leave, tell him something like this: "If you'll be available at three tomorrow, at that time I'll do my best to have the answers you're waiting for."

Before you see him again, you may find it helpful to study Chapter 11, "Making Return Calls Productive."

TIP 9: USE THE TELEPHONE WISELY TO SAVE TIME

For making appointments, expert salesmen use the telephone on direct calls only. Suppose Mr. Adams has been in touch with your office by telephone, newspaper coupon, magazine coupon, or personal visit, asking to have a sales representative call on him. That's a direct call from Mr. Adams. If it's necessary for you to telephone him to make an appointment to see him, don't hesitate to do so.

On the contrary, if Mr. Adams has not directly expressed an interest, but if your customer Mr. Baker has suggested that you call on Mr. Adams, this is an indirect inquiry. Where it's at all practicable, it's best *not* to telephone such a prospect to make the appointment for a sales demonstration. Instead, call in person at his home or office to make the appointment.

TIP 10: NEVER LET A CIGARETTE, CIGAR, OR PIPE LOSE YOU A SALE

The professional salesman doesn't usually smoke during a sales interview. He knows that he could smoke with perhaps a thousand prospects while attempting to obtain an order without jeopardizing a sale. He realizes, however, that in one or two cases in a thousand he can lose sales by smoking. He might spill ashes where he shouldn't or he could burn a hole in papers on a desk or in upholstery or a rug. So if he does smoke he does it before and after interviewing prospects.

He doesn't want to take even the one or two unnecessary chances in a thousand that might lose the sale.

TIP 11: COMMAND RESPECT AND DON'T BE RUSHED

Professional salesmen try not to let themselves be rushed. Now and then you'll find a prospect who thinks he's terrifically busy and important. He'll say something like this to you: "I can give you only three minutes to tell me all about your product. I've nine more salesmen to see who also want to submit estimates. Get going!"

Even if yours is among the lower-priced products, you are unwise to attempt to condense a one-hour sales presentation into three minutes. You're on the horns of a dilemma. You're wrong if you do what he asks, and you're wrong if you don't. This man probably won't choose the very lowest price—he'd be afraid to. But, out of a choice of nine or ten, he'd feel satisfied to choose the item third or fourth from the bottom of the list. Your likelihood of occupying that particular spot is purely chance.

Almost any salesman can think of an instance where he allowed himself to be rushed and yet obtained the order. If you remain twenty years in the specialty-selling field (where each sale is made to a new prospect), at least once in that time there'll be one prospect who will say, "I haven't time to listen to any story. Give me the order and let me sign it. I have an appointment and must get out of here right now."

Don't be misled! That man was probably sold by someone else before you ever saw him. Customers of that type are few and far between. It's difficult if not impossible for you to live on the income you make from such sources.

A handling that sometimes produces favorable results with a prospect who can "give you only three minutes" for your one-hour sales presentation is *not* to sell your product in that three minutes. Instead, what you try to do is to sell him the idea of giving you a reasonable length of time for your sales presentation.

128

SALES INTERVIEW SHOWING HOW TO
COMMAND RESPECT

You might tell the prospect, "Very well, sir, I'll do the best I can in that time. It actually takes about an hour for you to see with your own eyes why our equipment is the *lowest-cost* you can buy, regardless of initial purchase price. What do you want, Mr. Newton? To lay out the least amount of money right now, at the time of purchase—that is, to buy the cheapest unit—or do you want to invest in the equipment that, over the life of the product, will be far lower in cost than anything else you can buy? That's our story, Mr. Newton. We aren't the lowest-priced unit to buy, but we are by far the *lowest-cost* unit to *own*. By purchasing our equipment you'll obtain a far handsomer return on your money than you can in any other way. Does that interest you, Mr. Newton?

"If it does, wouldn't it pay you, on an investment of this magnitude, to take a little more of your time to see with your own eyes the features and the services that produce these results? You rarely get something for nothing, do you, Mr. Newton? You usually get just about what you pay for, don't you? Without spending the time to take the measurements and to do the required figuring to quote you a price, I can tell you that our initial outlay will probably be higher than that for other equipment. But over the life of the equipment, ours is by far the *lowest-cost* you can buy. Does that appeal to you at all?

"Yes, I can leave you a piece of literature to read. But you've had the experience with other items, I'm sure, of finding that the shoddiest merchandise is frequently promoted by the most luxurious and aristocratic and hard-hitting, all-claiming, and downright convincing literature, haven't you? It makes you wonder if they've taken some of the savings they make in cheapening their product and spent it on high-pressure advertising, doesn't it?

"We don't do that. Our literature is conservative. It's so concise that it simply doesn't properly cover all the features and services that make ours the lowest-cost unit to own. If we could find a piece of literature that would do this for us, Mr. Newton, we wouldn't need salesmen, would we? Would tomorrow at this same time be convenient for you to give our product the consideration I know you would like to?"

Should you unfortunately be greeted by a prospect who says, "In ten minutes I have to leave to catch a plane to Chicago," it is best to try for a *definite* substitute appointment and get out as rapidly as possible. You say, "I won't take any of your time *now*. Will you be able to see me Thursday at three instead?" Don't ask, "*When* can you see me instead?"

TIP 12: RECOGNIZE THE DIFFERENCE BETWEEN BEING ENTHUSIASTIC AND BEING EXCITABLE

The professional salesman takes it easy. This means that you should not be overbearing and that you should not shout at your prospect. You can lose sales by loud talk and by offensively aggressive manners. Certainly, once or twice during a sales presentation you can raise your voice or give the desk or table a thump when you emphasize an important point. But if your whole sales story is made up of loud talk and a continual drum roll of desk-thumpings, you'll antagonize your prospect and lose the sale.

Sometimes your interview with the prospect is conducted in an office with other people not far away. Be sure to make your presentation in such a manner that it will remain private between you two. Don't let it either disturb or inform others who may be nearby.

Enunciate clearly and talk loudly enough so that the prospect hears you. "Take it easy" doesn't mean that you should mumble and murmur and make a sloppy, careless sales presentation. "Take it easy" refers to the manner of your sales talk, not to the effort you put forth nor to the time you spend in your sales endeavors. It isn't intended to encourage anyone in the belief that he can coast along, do little work, and garner a huge income.

TIP 13: DON'T LET AN INTERVIEW BE TOO LONG

Expert salesmen have learned that a recess will often pay off. In Chapter 3 you were informed that you should hew to the line, keep to your subject, use straight-line selling. There are two circumstances under which it may be advisable to modify this instruction.

The first case is that of an *extraordinarily long sales presenta-*

tion. Suppose that for two hours you've been giving your sales story and that you're just beyond the half-way point. You sense that the prospect is finding the going tough. He's getting groggy, yet you believe you've not obtained sufficient commitments to justify trying for the close. Here it may be well to call a recess. You deliberately break off the sales story and draw out the prospect on a subject entirely foreign to it. Get him to do the talking. You be the listener. Continue this for ten or fifteen minutes or more.

Then, just as deliberately as you veered out of it, turn back to the major purpose of your call, with an *attempt at a close* as the springboard. Your technique might be something like this: "What you say is most interesting, Mr. Perkins. But it's a long way from the subject of the evening, isn't it? You've said you like the fixtures and the walls and the floors and the lighting we're going to install in your new bathroom, haven't you? Why not put your name right here, and we'll get the whole matter cleared up and you won't have any further worry about it?"

Since the prospect's guard is down at this point, in a good proportion of the cases he'll sign. Remember, it's foolish to spend the time on the recess unless you try to use its as a springboard to catapult into the order. If you don't get the order at this point, you still have more features to present in your sales story, with other opportunities for making the close.

The second occasion on which it will pay you to call a recess is when the prospect becomes drowsy and begins to nod. This may occur early in your sales presentation—five or ten minutes after you begin—or it may happen later. It even may occur oftener than once. It may not necessarily be your fault, but rather the result of a sleepless night or a heavy meal. Regardless of the cause, your story will be ineffective if it falls on deaf ears. It's essential that the prospect be awakened. The surest and simplest way to do this—short of shaking him vigorously— is to start him talking.

To draw him out, change the subject from your product to his hobby or his home or his business or his family. Then sit back and listen. He should talk for at least several minutes, perhaps longer.

When you think he's wide enough awake, bring the conversation back to your product and continue your story from

131

where you left off, with a brief summary of what went before. If you've previously obtained several commitments and given reasons for buying your product, you can of course try for the order. If, however, the recess has come early in your sales presentation, a try for the order at this point may be unwise.

TIP 14: SUMMARIZE FREQUENTLY ON FIRST AND ON FOLLOW-UP CALLS

Expert salesmen summarize frequently. Let's assume that you've divided your sales presentation as follows:

1. At least three reasons why the prospect should buy the type of product or service you're selling.
2. At least three reasons why he should buy your product rather than any competing brand in the same field.
3. At least three reasons why he should buy your product NOW.

After every three major points, give a summary. In this summary include all that has gone before. Make your summaries brief. Use diplomacy and tact, so that you don't offend your prospect by casting doubts on his intelligence or bore him by exact word-for-word repetitions. Try for at least one smooth recommitment after the summary of each section. If you've been using pencil and paper, as suggested earlier in this chapter, summarizing won't be difficult.

The reason why frequent summaries are necessary is that *human memory is fallible.* You know the story, but if you want it to remain in your prospect's memory sufficiently long for you to get the order, you'll have to emphasize or repeat again and again. One way of doing this is to have the prospect participate. Another way is to obtain commitments. The final, and highly important, way of impressing your story upon the prospect is by frequent summaries.

A sales interview illustrating the summary technique:

A typical summary might run something like this: "Well, Mr. Ritter, up to this point we've covered the following three reasons why people buy Metropole automatic heating equipment: first, to save money by reducing expenses; second, to eliminate drudgery; third, to bring greater comfort. They're all good, sound reasons, aren't they, Mr. Ritter? And I believe they appeal to you, don't they? In addition, we've covered the following three exclusive features of our equipment: one, self-lubrication; two, one moving part; three, automatic, trouble-free controls. That's real engineering, isn't it, Mr. Ritter? You see now why our unit saves so much money and is so dependable, don't you?"

If you feel that you've obtained enough prior commitments, together with additional recommitments at the summary, try for the close at this point. Remember, the summary is not only useful to impress your story firmly upon the prospect but it's also a strong auxiliary technique when moving into the close.

TIP 15: ALWAYS LET THE BUYER KNOW YOU WANT THE ORDER

Expert salesmen, if questioned, tell the prospect they're there to get an order. Someone has described sales technique as an attempt by the salesman to maneuver the prospect into dropping his guard, so that the former can deliver a knockout wallop. If, accordingly, you walk into the prospect's home or office and blatantly announce, "I'm here to get an order!" he'll put up his guard and keep it up, and you'll have little chance of making the sale.

It's interesting and helpful to know, however, that the same announcement, properly worded and correctly timed, actually helps lower the prospect's guard. Suppose, for example, that you're far enough along in your sales presentation, and have obtained sufficient commitments, to try for a close. And suppose that the prospect responds with a statement along the following lines: "Why, Mr. Salesman, you told me you wanted me to see some of the features of your equipment. And here you are asking for an order! I didn't think you were going to try to sell me anything."

In this illustration we can ignore the question of whether or not he is serious in this statement. The important fact to remember is that now and then a prospect may appear to express surprise, or even resentment, when you try to close.

Sales Interview Demonstrating How to **Let the Buyer Know** You Want the Order:

An answer that has proven successful in such cases runs something like this: "Mr. Stoddard, Mrs. Stoddard and you have a very attractive, comfortable home here. From that I infer that you do your work well where you're employed, or else you couldn't afford to keep up a home like this. I respect you for doing a good job. You, on the other hand, wouldn't think much of me if I didn't do my work well. I'm a salesman. And a salesman is supposed to try for the order, isn't he? If I didn't, you wouldn't respect me, would you?"

You'll find that, after a statement such as this, you can usually try again and again for the order at appropriate intervals, without fear of further protests or resentment.

TIP 16: REMOVE YOUR COMPETITOR FROM THE RUNNING—WHEN POSSIBLE

Expert salesmen take catalogues, if possible. You'll sometimes see quite a collection of competitive literature on the customer's table or desk after you've obtained the order. It's a good idea to try to get such catalogues, if you can do so by a casual approach.

Here's an example: "Mr. Taylor, I don't imagine you'll have any more use for that printed matter. If you're going to throw it away, I'll be glad to dispose of it for you, if you'll let me. Frankly, I'd like to glance through it before I discard it. The more I read the other fellow's literature, the more my own product appeals to me."

If you can't obtain the literature by a casual approach, give up the attempt.

There are two advantages in your having the competitive literature after you obtain the order. The first is that you can study it and learn what arguments your competitors are using, and you can devise methods of combating their claims on future sales. The second advantage is that you eliminate the possibility of having your customer pick up a piece of it after he's purchased from you and become fascinated by some entrancing illustration or tantalizing claim, making it necessary for you to return and resell him in order to save the sale.

TIP 17: CHECK YOURSELF PERIODICALLY— TO IMPROVE CONTINUALLY

If you want to be an expert salesman, check yourself frequently against the key review points at the end of each chapter. Do this once a month for three months after you first read this book. If you don't know the answer to a particular question, reread the appropriate portion of the chapter several times and attempt to put its suggestions into use in your next sales presentations.

Repeat this check-up at the end of three months, and after that every six months, for the rest of your selling career. In spite of sincerity and earnestness on your part, you'll find that carelessness will tend to creep into your sales activity. These repeated check-ups will help you guard against acquiring undesirable selling habits.

Should your sales productivity drop, periodic check-ups will help you discover the reason for the decline, and you can then take remedial action. Sales managers, or other sales executives, can use the test questions on weak salesmen or those with declining volume to determine where they need strengthening.

This means that every time you lose an order you should go over the key review questions carefully and determine the cause of your failure. In this manner you can guard against establishing bad selling habits. These key review questions should be used not only to strengthen your selling power but also to help you continue to be a successful salesman.

KEY REVIEW POINTS FOR
SELF-IMPROVEMENT

Give an example of emphasizing the positive and eliminating the negative in selling.

Can you think of another example of this?

What is meant by "negative selling"?

When an unpleasant idea must be brought up, what can you do with it to make it acceptable?

Give an example of honest and logical magnification of savings.

Give a similar example of shrinking the cost.

Which is better, to bring out the bad news at the very beginning or to delay it until the end?

How can you bring your prospect to the boiling point and keep him there?

How can you focus your standardized sales demonstration on the key objection?

When should you have the order pad ready? Why?

How can you make it easy for the prospect to sign?

Should you take each prospect through every page of your sales album?

How should you use your sales helps?

How do successful salesmen use paper and pencil to help themselves?

How can you use paper and pencil in summarizing?

Where signatures of both husband and wife are required, should you attempt to sell one without the other?

Where you can't escape from giving your sales presentation to one half of the husband-wife team, what should you do?

When you have to impart information that may sting or smart, what should you do?

What is meant by "clinching" a prospect?

Why shouldn't you use a clincher if the order cannot be signed at that time?

Explain the difference between a direct and an indirect inquiry from a prospect.

What is the advantage of a personal call by you for making an appointment for a sales demonstration?

What kind of merchandise is adaptable for telephone selling?

What kinds of prospects can be sold on the telephone?

What kind of merchandise is poorly adapted for telephone selling?

Should you smoke when making your sales presentation? Why not?

How can you answer the prospect who says, "I can give you only three minutes to tell me all about your product?"

What can you do if the prospect says, "In ten minutes I have to leave to catch a plane to Chicago"?

What is meant by the advice, "Take it easy"?

On what two occasions may it be advisable to have a recess in your sales presentation?

What should you do at the end of a recess during a long sales presentation?

Why are frequent summaries helpful?

For what part of the sale is the summary a strong auxiliary technique?

What can you answer if the prospect expresses surprise, or possibly resentment, when you try to close?

Why is it desirable to take competitive literature with you, if your customer will let you have it without protest when you've closed a sale and are about to leave?

Why should you check yourself frequently against the test questions at each chapter's end?

How should you use these questions?

How long should you continue periodic check-ups?

Little things make the
expert salesman

Chapter 10

Adding Plus Know-How to Your Selling Effort

Sell yourself, not just your product
Know your product or service **thoroughly**
Be **businesslike**
Add the **plus know-how** to your selling
What about **your promotion** or **raise**

USUALLY, TO obtain an order, you must sell yourself in addition to selling your product. "How can I sell myself?" is a universal problem—not only for those who have chosen to specialize in the profession of salesmanship. Physicians and surgeons, ministers of the Gospel, lawyers, accountants, teachers, merchants, advertising men, laundry men, newspaper reporters, columnists, editors, carpenters, painters, bricklayers, plumbers—all need to sell themselves, their ideas, and their accomplishments.

Don't Sell Only Your Product—Sell Yourself

The quickest and surest way for anyone to sell himself is to *do his work well.*

Stop and think. Don't *you* admire and respect, and usually *like,* the man who does his work skillfully, whatever his line of endeavor may be?

Your work is selling, isn't it? To sell yourself, therefore, concentrate on doing a good job of selling your product or service.

By doing this you'll be making a friend of your prospect, without spending time on subjects foreign to your product or service. Of course you'll dress neatly and keep yourself clean and well groomed. Naturally you'll be courteous and honest and decent. And you'll handle the prospect on the basis of the Golden Rule. Moreover, you'll carefully follow the suggestions in the last chapter and avoid antagonizing your prospect.

Have an Extensive Knowledge of Your Product or Service

Regardless of what else you may do and regardless of how pleasant and charming your personality may be, it will be difficult to sell your product—and, in the process, yourself—unless you have a comprehensive knowledge of your product and its uses. This is particularly true if you're trying to sell a basic or standard commodity also sold by competitors whose companies' reputations are as high as yours and who offer the same prices, terms, delivery, and quality of material as you do —or if you're trying to sell a product or service at a price higher than that of your major competitors.

For example, consider soda ash, which is a staple chemical sold by many manufacturers of unquestioned standing. As a salesman of such a product, if you have a sufficiently extensive knowledge of it to be able to suggest to your prospect a way of reducing the quantity he requires or of securing more effective results from his present quantity or of using it in additional ways, then you're on the inside track to getting his orders.

Conversely, if you lack knowledge of your product or its uses and are unable to conceal your ignorance (in the manner suggested in Chapter 2), then you may very well be a dead duck.

The moral is that it will pay you well to *know as much as possible about your product and its uses.* You can't know too much. And you should be alert to learn new uses and new facts about it as long as you're a salesman. After you've acquired all this vast knowledge, however, be sure not to cram ALL of it down the throat of each prospect. If you do, you'll probably talk yourself out of more orders than you close.

Many salesmen of large-volume items carry on a lengthy campaign of entertainment and personal association and friendship before they attempt to make a sales presentation. Other salesmen spend a large share of the time allotted for their interview in chatting in a social manner with the prospect. They discuss such matters as golf, college, vacation spots, personalities, baseball, and war experiences, in an endeavor not only to establish a mutuality of interest but to sell themselves. Often they find themselves eased out of the prospect's home or office in a most friendly manner—in fact, they may have become seemingly good friends—with very little time spent on product presentation. That, in such cases, is deferred until a later interview.

Meanwhile, a competitive salesman sees the same prospect. This competitor gives a strong, hard-hitting sales presentation without spending any appreciable amount of the valuable time allotted to him on social chitchat. He further adds several cogent reasons why the prospect should sign NOW. Frequently the prospect *does* sign the competitor's order blank. Amazingly, he thinks the competitor is a splendid fellow—"all business, certainly knows what he's talking about. I'd like to have a man like that working for me."

When the chitchat salesman returns for his second call he's greeted something like this: "Hello, Jim! I'm sure glad to see you. I've been looking forward to that golf date with you this Friday. I know you won't mind if I tell you that I've already had to place the order elsewhere. But we'll still play golf together next Friday, and the drinks will be on me."

We repeat: the surest, quickest, and most profitable way of selling yourself is to *do a workmanlike job of selling your product*. Those minutes with the prospect are golden. It's best for you not to risk wasting them. Utilize them for a strong, persuasive sales presentation. This is the manner in which you'll sell yourself. And often you'll get the order then and there. The entertaining and social intercourse (if necessary in some cases) should come *after* the sale has been made and the transaction completed by delivery and installation of the product. Although in some cases a salesman may never get a chance to talk about his products unless he contacts his prospect via the golfing or entertainment route.

Add the Plus Know-How to Your Selling

For that extra finesse in selling, develop and master the following "plus know-how" and put it into operation whenever you can.

ENCOURAGE A PROSPECT TO TALK

If you had a machine that could read people's minds, you could make millions of dollars, couldn't you? When talking to prospects, you'd know what they were thinking. With this tremendous advantage in your contact with them, making your fortune would be easy.

You've probably already realized that you can read an individual's mind without any mechanical device. All you need do is to encourage him to talk. If he never says a word, you haven't much chance of learning what he's thinking, have you? His conversation, attentively absorbed by you, will give you a clue to his thoughts.

Don't Give the Prospect a "Snow Job"

Have you ever heard a man say, "I didn't get the order but I sure snowed that prospect under! I didn't let him say a word"? And then there's the jubilant salesman who comes back and relates, "I certainly told off that prospect." Salesmen should be pitied who believe that they should do all the talking. Their practice ensures that they'll never learn what the prospect is thinking. And thus they'll also have little opportunity of acting on that valuable information.

The best sale is often made with the least talk.

One way of restricting your conversation is to quit talking when you've made the sale. Don't talk yourself into an order and then out of it!

AVOID TIME-WASTING CONVERSATION

Another way to limit your words is to stick to the subject. Don't drag in extraneous matters. They're time-wasters, and besides they confuse.

After you've succeeded in encouraging him to talk, you may find it necessary to keep the prospect on the pertinent subject by proper questions and comments. You can't afford to spend the time he's allotted you by listening to his views on the baseball situation, for example, when you're actually in his office to get an order for steel girders. So long as a prospect is talking *about your product and company and service* or is describing *his particular problem*, you advance the sale by *keeping quiet*. In such cases, don't attempt to take the conversational lead away from him. He's selling himself.

The substitute, then, for that magical mind-reading machine is the secret, "DON'T TALK TOO MUCH." Encourage your potential buyer to talk. *Observe and listen to him.* Soon you'll have a good idea of what he's thinking. When you do, act on that information.

BE TRUTHFUL—BUT DON'T TELL EVERYTHING YOU KNOW

Anything you say should be truthful. Yet you don't need to tell everything you know. Answer questions, but keep your replies as brief as you can without sacrificing clarity. Don't attempt to bluff. Above all, don't lie—or even mislead by innuendo.

It's amazing, but true, that many prospects are suspicious of salesmen. Countless people are convinced that salesmen are liars and crooks. Often you'll be asked questions to which the prospect already knows the answer. If you give the incorrect reply, your goose is cooked. You've lost his confidence. He's proved that he's right and that you're another of those lying, crooked salesmen. There's no way of gluing together the eggs that you've cracked. You have no chance of getting back into his good graces. You're through!

So, whatever you say, be truthful. Answer briefly but satisfactorily.

You don't need to drag in elaborations and expansions of the answer that might be harmful to the sale. Suppose Mr. Garlington, your air-conditioning prospect, has asked, "What refrigerant does your unit use?" When you reply, "We use nontoxic Freon," you lose more than you gain if you voluntarily add, "We've chosen a nontoxic refrigerant so that if there should be a leak neither you nor any of your employees would be harmed."

You'll note that by this addition you've put a retarding idea into Mr. Garlington's mind. You've set up for yourself one more obstacle that you'll have to remove before you can close him. And *you* did it! *He* didn't. Whose team are you on, anyway?

SAY "I DON'T KNOW" WHEN YOU DON'T

If a prospect asks you a question and you don't know the answer, it's unwise to fake a reply. In such cases, you will build confidence if you frankly tell him that you don't know but that you'll find out for him. Then he'll be more inclined to believe you when you make other statements with which you are familiar. A good way of handling a question that has baffled you is to answer like this: "I'm awfully glad you asked that question, Mr. Olds, because it gives me an opportunity of learning something additional about my product. You're the first man I've met, in all the time I've been selling power mowers, with sufficient intelligence and technical background to ask me this question. I don't know the answer, although I might hazard a guess. Rather than do that, I'm going to make a note of your question and take it up with our engineering department and get an answer for you."

(The observant reader will note that this is a variation of a similar example given in Chapter 2.)

USE THE PRINTED WORD TO CREATE CONFIDENCE

One of your toughest problems is to instill in prospects' minds confidence in yourself. An action that helps build this confidence is to let them see. In addition to offering to demonstrate working models, showroom displays, and actual installations, when you're asked technical questions in regard to capacity, performance, etc., it's effective to point out the information in your manual and have the prospect read it for himself. "There are our specifications in black and white, Mr. Irwin," you can say, putting your manual in front of him; "I'm not asking you to rely on my unsupported claims."

SPEED YOUR SELLING WITH MORE SHOWING

If you have a model or a demonstration unit of your equipment that you can take with you, put it into the prospect's hands. It's one of your strongest sales tools to add realism to your sales story. Next to the actual unit in sales power are photographs, charts and diagrams, testimonial letters, and finally, pencil and paper.

Taking your prospect to see actual installations in customers' homes or buildings or factories, where he can talk to satisfied users, or to visit your showroom display, is hard-hitting, effective selling, if it can be done readily and smoothly. This action may have a twofold liability, however: first, you frequently have difficulty in persuading the prospect to accompany you; second, the visit to showroom or installation often delays the closing of the order. For these two reasons, therefore, you're advised to take your prospect to your showroom display or to see actual installations only if other methods of securing the order do not prove effective and if you are reasonably confident that this action won't retard expediting a sale.

ALLAYING THEIR FEARS

Many prospects, including a large number of those who need it most, are suspicious of financing. They've read or heard about people who've been gypped by unscrupulous juggling of rates. You can allay their fears and further build confidence in yourself by putting your finance chart in front of them and asking them to help you by checking your figures, so that you "are sure not to overcharge them accidentally."

Letting prospects read testimonial letters from users—or, better yet, talk to actual users—is another confidence-builder. You can add tremendously to the power of testimonial letters by including photographs of installations coordinated with the appropriate letters.

CUSTOMERS DON'T WANT CLAIMS— THEY WANT PROOF

When a prospect has listened to two or three sales presentations or has read advertising of two or three competitive products, you'll find that his mind is often a maze of what he calls "conflicting claims." Should you make a strong statement about your product, this type of prospect may brush it aside with a statement like this: "Other makes claim the same feature."

Here is your opportunity to capitalize on this viewpoint. Encourage him in the belief that the competitors have simply *made claims,* while in your case he will *see* with his own eyes the benefits your product brings.

TOO MUCH PROOF MAY BE AS BAD AS TOO LITTLE

If you try to outdo other salesmen with proof and more proof, many prospects will become less convinced, because so much proof may be indicative that it is necessary to cover up certain shortcomings.

Rather than offering too much proof and outclaiming competitors, you can say something like this: "Mr. Loomis, you're quite right. The other manufacturers are trying frantically to catch up with us. Some of them are making *claims*—just as

144

you say—that they have some of our exclusive features. I'm not trying to make any *claims* about our features. Instead, I'm attempting to let you *see* with your own eyes just how our outboard motor brings you these exclusive advantages. Instead of listening to a lot of *claims,* as you have been doing, wouldn't you rather *see* with your own eyes, and judge for yourself, the benefits we bring?"

How to Sell Yourself for a Promotion or a Raise

When you're selling an idea, such as a raise or a promotion for yourself, you can lower the boss' resistance by mentioning his objections and answering them in your approach.* Here's an example:

"Mr. Jarvis, I know that, because of the pressure of taxes and government regulations on the one hand, and the constantly increasing costs of doing business on the other hand, it's very difficult for management to produce a satisfactory margin of profit. I've been looking around, and I wonder if you'd be interested in the sales and profit potential of this electronic fire detector that I've found.

"It's an item that fits into our line and can be sold to our present customers. Our margin on it would be 10 per cent higher than on any other merchandise we carry. The manufacturer is willing to allow us a sixty-day period during which we can give its potential a thorough test. For that length of time he'll honor our orders by direct shipment, so that we won't need to invest any money in merchandise until we've satisfied ourselves that we can make a go of it. I've been in touch with several of our customers and, from the response received from them, I'm quite sure that I can guarantee $10,000 of business in the first two weeks. I think it should increase after that. I wonder if you'd give me permission to try this out and see what I can do with it. Also, if it does go over, I wonder if it's asking too much for you to consider me as the head of the department."

Now that you've learned some methods of selling yourself, you are more than ever ready to do a positive job of selling. In Part III you will learn how to use your time more productively.

* Be sure not to mention negative ideas that your employer typically would not think of, or you may be putting an idea into his head that would not occur to him.

SUMMARY THOUGHT-PROVOKERS

In this chapter you've seen that the surest way of selling yourself is to do your work well—that is, to be competent and businesslike and thorough in selling your product. You've been cautioned not to talk too much during a sales presentation. To build the prospect's confidence in you, you've been advised to tell the truth. If you don't know the answer to his questions, you were told to inform him that you'll find out. To further build confidence, it was suggested that you impress upon him that you're letting him *see* with his own eyes. Thus he isn't relying on just *"claims"* from you, but more on proof, demonstration, illustration, and explanation.

KEY REVIEW POINTS FOR SELF-IMPROVEMENT

What is the surest way of selling yourself?

How can you read the prospect's mind?

Describe two ways in which you can limit your own conversation.

After you've learned what the prospect is thinking, what should you do?

Why should you tell the truth?

Should you attempt to bluff the prospect?

Why should your answers be brief?

When the prospect asks you a question to which you don't know the answer, what should you do?

Why should you let the prospect see your model or demonstrator and actually handle it and work it, if possible?

What are the advantages of taking your prospect to actual installations, to users, and to your showroom display?

What are the disadvantages?

How can you handle a prospect who says, "Other makes *claim* the same advantage?"

> Don't leave your prospects **vulnerable**
>   to competition!
> Sell **yourself**
> Sell your **product** or **service**
> Sell your **company policies**
> Sell your **leadership**

Chapter 11

Making Return Calls Productive

The importance of the **first call**
Try calling **again**
Leave the way open to **return**
Special handling for the return calls
Transitional phrases for **recommitments**

Make the First Call Pay Off

The first call is important. When we speak of the "first call" we mean, of course, the call on which you first go through a sales demonstration with the prospect. That's when he obtains his initial impression of you and your product. That's also when you first bring him from freezing to boiling and when, by proper procedure, in many cases you close him then and there. For—unless you're already at the boiling point—you can increase your percentage of one-call sales by improving your sales technique. In addition, that's the time you can make a definite appointment for a return call in those cases where you don't get the order on this initial interview.

Too many salesmen assume a prospect won't buy on the first call, and they prove themselves right by not asking him to do so.

Make Repeat Calls

If you don't get the order on the first call, try again. Try several times, until the prospect has bought. Neglecting to do this means that in many cases you're setting him up for a competitive sale. You've gained attention and have probably stimulated his desire for your type of merchandise. So when your competitor shows up, he can capitalize on your previous efforts

—unless you make return calls. Remember, no matter how skillfully you try, not every sale is made on the first call. (You will, of course, save time and money for both the prospect and yourself if you're sufficiently competent to close the sale during your first presentation, thus eliminating the necessity for return calls.)

The habit of making return calls will give you another advantage over the so-called born salesman, who frequently judges a prospect incorrectly when actually his own sales technique is at fault.

When you try again for the commitments that you didn't get on the first attempt, it will be decidedly helpful to mention some achievements that you didn't stress previously—this in addition to making sure that your second presentation is a better and smoother technical production than the first.

Even where you get a brusque brush-off when trying to interview a prospect, it will pay you to try again to see him. Perhaps he really *is* busy. After all, he must have a good many things to do in addition to talking to salesmen all day long. Maybe on the next visit he'll be under less pressure and in a more jovial mood.

State a Specific Reason for Repeat Calls

If you see the end of your interview approaching (whether it's the first call or any later call), and you haven't obtained the order, be sure to instill firmly in the prospect's mind the idea that you'll return, TOGETHER WITH A SPECIFIC REASON FOR THAT RETURN.

It isn't enough to say, "I'll be back on Thursday, Mr. Trent, to see what you decide." If you say that, you're likely not to get very far on your Thursday visit. At that time Mr. Trent may tell you, "I haven't decided anything as yet, Mr. Salesman. But I'll let you know when I do." And you're eased swiftly and smoothly out of his office or home. If you try to give him some additional sales features or to review those you previously used, he'll frequently say, "I know your story. You told it to me when you were here last week. I'll keep your product in mind when I make my decision."

To guard against this type of response, make a date with the prospect before you leave him, giving a definite reason and a specific program for your follow-up call. Here are some examples:

"Mr. Trent, when I come back on Thursday I'll bring the scale model, which wasn't available today. It will be very helpful to you in visualizing the situation and in assisting you in solving your problem."

"Mr. Trent, I'm sorry I must leave before we can go into the story of the development of this type of equipment. It's something that you should know before making your decision. I'll be able to go into it with you when I see you on Thursday."

LEAVE A PROSPECT WITH A REASON
TO SEE YOU AGAIN

Every good salesman carries lists of users and testimonial letters in his sales kit. Suppose, however, that you feel that your prospect may be particularly swayed by users in his own line of business and testimonial letters from them. You're sure that you can obtain a good selection of them by Thursday. So you say, "Mr. Trent, when I return on Thursday I'll have something new and different to let you see, which I think will interest you a great deal. Unfortunately, it wasn't available today." (You'll notice that you're giving a specific reason for your return, even if you haven't spelled out, letter by letter, just what it is you're going to present at that time.)

How to Handle Return Calls

COMMAND RESPECT ON RETURN CALLS

Salesmen who handle repeat merchandise and who are attempting to establish repeat customers find it frequently pays them to call on a prospect often enough to become his friend. If you can't become his friend, at least command his respect. Don't sacrifice respect to make friends, and thus fail to make a sale. If a prospect ever wants to change his source of merchandise, salesmen he respects are high on the call list.

REFRESH THE PROSPECT'S MEMORY

When you see the prospect on a return call—whether it's the second call or the twenty-second—your problem is to heat him up again to the boiling point, so that you can make a close. You've seen in Chapter 3 how you can keep him hot. You can reheat him in the same manner—by giving (more briefly than in your original presentation):

1. Three reasons for buying merchandise of your type;
2. Three reasons for buying your brand rather than another brand;
3. Three reasons for buying NOW.

Sure, you've given him that before. And it's old stuff to him. That's true. But it isn't so old and familiar to the prospect as it is to you. Remember, you have only one subject on your mind—your product. He, however, has thousands of other subjects to occupy his attention in addition to the story of your merchandise. Your story has become fuzzy in his memory.

If you know what you said on the first call, it is easier to telescope such points in review on a second call. This is another significant advantage of planned selling strategies, as you are not nearly so apt to be inconsistent in what you say to a prospect on follow-up calls.

Remember, too, that between your visits the prospect may have interviewed several of your competitors. Which feature belongs to which brand may have become hazy in his mind. Every time you visit the prospect, you should help him sharpen his focus on your product.

In refreshing his memory, it's important to be diplomatic. Try to have something new to bring up at each interview. You may have to give him old facts, but you can give them with new phrasing, can't you?

EXAMPLE OF HOW TO REVIEW WHAT YOU COVERED IN A PREVIOUS INTERVIEW:

Most prospects will not resent a review introduced by one of the following: "I'm sure, Mr. Ulmer, you remember . . ." or, "You'll recall, Mr. Ulmer, that during our last interview we covered . . ." or, possibly better still, "I remember, Mr. Ulmer, on my last call you asked . . ." or "you stated . . ."

KEEP THE BUYER SOLD ON YOUR BRAND
AND YOUR COMPANY

On return calls to established customers, it's wise to keep the buyer sold on your company and your brand. During your absence he's probably been wooed by the appealing stories of salesmen of competitive products. If you don't keep him sold meanwhile, this may happen between your visits.

Return or follow-up calls are made for the purpose of securing an order. Therefore it's essential that you obtain commitments *during each of such return calls*. This holds true even though you've gotten commitments during the previous call or calls. By trying for commitments on each return call, you greatly improve your chances of closing the sale at that time, because obtaining commitments during your review of your sales demonstration helps thaw the prospect and again moves him upward toward the boiling point.

Moreover, as you try for these recommitments, you gain a quick and almost continuous indicator as to your progress. If the prospect gives you the commitments, he's warming up. But if he doesn't give them to you (either actively or passively), you'd better check over your story and your technique and improve them.

Illustrative Transitional Phrases for Getting Recommitments

Of course you'll try for the order on each follow-up call after you've asked at least six committing questions.

To smooth over the process of getting recommitments, try introducing them with something like the following:

"I believe that during our previous interview, Mr. Voorhees, you liked the quietness of our unit, didn't you?"

"And its simplicity appealed to you, didn't it?"

"When I was here before, this compact construction attracted you, didn't it?"

"If I'm not mistaken, the easy-to-clean finish was one of the features that you appreciated, wasn't it, Mr. Voorhees?"

An ability to keep yourself supplied with all the prospects you need, coupled with an ability to sell a satisfactory proportion of them, will give you true economic security.

The next chapter, therefore, tells you about "Finding Prospects."

KEY REVIEW POINTS FOR
SELF-IMPROVEMENT

Why is the first call important?

Why should you try again if you don't get the order on the first call?

Why should you try again when you get a brush-off on a prospecting call?

Where a return call (also known as a follow-up call) is planned, why should you give a definite reason and a specific program to your prospect for this return call?

What should you be sure to review on each return call? Why?

What is the usual purpose of follow-up or return calls?

Why should you get recommitments on repeat calls?

Make return calls
for greater **payoff!**

Chapter 12

Finding Prospects

LET'S ASSUME that you're an experienced salesman. Having gone through the preceding eleven chapters of this book, you have been reminded of a number of selling techniques and sales strategies obtained from years of experience. Yet, even though you know how to sell various kinds of products and you can distinguish between different types of buyers and individuals, your sales volume will be disappointingly low, *unless you have an adequate supply of prospects*.

Prospects Are Opportunities to Sell

Obviously, before you make a sale, you must have someone to whom to sell—that is, you must have a prospect. The more prospects you obtain, the more opportunities you'll have to make sales.

Here's another important area in which it's not difficult to surpass many salesmen who operate largely by instinct and chance. If you organize and use a definite plan of prospecting, you can readily accumulate far more prospects.

To cite an extreme example, suppose you've collected ten prospects while another salesman whom you know has acquired only one during the same period. Then you'll have ten opportunities of making a sale to his one. Even though at the beginning you may be weaker than the other salesman in knowledge of your product and in selling skill, with ten prospects to his one you've started to cut him down to size, if not to surpass him. With study of your product and with the actual experience of putting this knowledge into practice in the field, you'll quickly begin to exceed the born salesman's production.

Suspects, Prospects, and Customers Defined

Suspects are those who need or would like to have your type of product and who are financially able to make the purchase, but whose intention of buying it at this time hasn't definitely crystallized.

Prospects are people who need or who would like to have your type of product, who are financially able to make the purchase, and who are actually going to buy it (from you or from some other salesman).

Customers are the ones who have already bought it.

This chapter gives you some specific, practical ideas on obtaining prospects. Studying the other chapters in the book should help you improve and strengthen the selling methods you use on those prospects.

Your prospects will come from either your company (from its advertising, promotion, and other such activities), from your own efforts, or from a combination of both of these sources.

Why You Can't Stop Prospecting

If you join an organization where you are to sell to one hundred established customers and you don't add any new ones, you'll have less than one hundred to call on at the end of the year. People die. Customers go out of business; they retire or sell out to others who have their own sources of supply. Moreover, regardless of how careful and conscientious the service that your company gives, there'll be one or two customers a year who'll leave because they feel they've been poorly treated.

So, even if your company supplies you with established customers or with prospects obtained from their various advertising campaigns, canvassers hired for the purpose, or other sources, it's still wise to organize your work so that you regularly spend a definite amount of time each week securing new prospects. Naturally, you'll accept gladly, and try to sell, every prospect that is handed to you. But should the returns from advertising decline, if you know how to dig up your own prospects you have a valuable asset. A good time to learn how to get prospects is when you don't need to do it.

Suggestions for Prospecting

MAKE UP A LIST OF HIGH-GRADE SUSPECTS AND CALL ON THEM

Many salesmen make an excellent living calling on everybody in their territory, regardless of need, occupation, or income. However, if you pick out logical suspects for your prospects and call on them instead of on "everybody in the city directory," you can save time. If you're a salesman of diesel locomotives, you call on railroad companies and perhaps some of the larger construction companies and mining, lumbering, and manufacturing concerns. If you're a salesman of room air conditioners, you try to find the names and home addresses of occupants of air-conditioned business buildings. When you see these gentlemen in their homes, you tell them that they and their wives can have the same comfort and health at home as that enjoyed in the office: "It's silly to be cool and comfortable all day and then swelter all night, isn't it? Doesn't your wife deserve the same consideration that you get?"

The salesman should bear in mind that people already owning gas- or oil-heating units will also be in the market for replacements sooner or later. Perhaps some will decide they want a central heating unit or that they prefer gas rather than the oil they have been using.

ASK YOUR SATISFIED CUSTOMERS
TO RECOMMEND PROSPECTS

The salesman of life insurance or investments makes a particular point of calling on those people to whom he has been recommended by satisfied customers, and on parents of new babies, on men who have just been promoted, and on people who have recently received legacies.

MAKE A LIST OF PRESENT OWNERS, USERS,
OR BUYERS OF YOUR PRODUCT OR SERVICE

All such people as those indicated above are high-grade suspects. With a little thought, in any business you can prepare a list of suspects for that particular merchandise. From these you can separate "live" prospects by using questions such as those given below. Remember that it's from "live" prospects that sales are obtained.

CONVERT SUSPECTS INTO PROSPECTS

In selling, of course your major effort should be directed toward converting prospects into customers. But if you're wise, you'll use a certain amount of your time to convert suspects into prospects.

QUESTIONS FOR SIFTING PROSPECTS
FROM SUSPECTS

Here are some samples of questions that have been successfully used to sift out prospects from among suspects:

"Would you like to save $50,000 a year in your production department? Would you be available on Wednesday at eleven to discuss what I have in mind?"

"Would you have time at three this afternoon to hear how you can get quicker deliveries and better service on your purchases of ball bearings?"

"Could you spare some time on Friday at two to hear about the newest development in titanium alloys?"

"Have you and your husband already arranged for your son's college education? If not, would you like to hear an almost painless method of providing funds for putting him through college?"

"Do you like to shovel coal and carry out ashes? Wouldn't

you be glad to be rid of the drudgery of furnace-tending? Would you and your husband be available Thursday evening at eight for me to take some measurements and give you a free estimate on our automatic gas heating unit?"

"I'm not here to talk to you *now*. I just wonder when you can spare two minutes to answer a question. Would Tuesday at two be a convenient time for me to come back and take a few measurements and give you a free estimate on reducing your heating bill and giving you a safer and more comfortable home with self-storing aluminum storm windows?"

WATCH FOR PROSPECTS

Suppose you're in the midst of an air-conditioning presentation to two business executives. One of them turns to the other and says, "This would be a godsend for that restaurant where we had lunch today, wouldn't it, Joe?"

Joe replies, "I'll say it would!"

In a case like this, the salesman is sometimes so intent upon carrying through his sales presentation in its logical sequence that he ignores these remarks. If you don't wish to interrupt the progress of your sales story, what you should do is write the word "restaurant" on the pad in front of you. Later, when there's a suitable break in your demonstration, you can ask, "What were the name and address of that restaurant where you lunched today? I can give you the same comfort during your meals as you'll have here in the office."

If you're alert, you'll hear many more such prospect suggestions dropped by people with whom you are conversing. There are many instances where, before your arrival, the prospect has talked to his friends about his intended purchase. Some of them may have remarked, "I'm thinking of installing air conditioning too. Let me know how you make out."

PROSPECT DURING A SALES INTERVIEW

If you try for prospects only at the end of your presentation, you'll find that many of those who don't buy will tell you, "Yes, I know two or three others who're waiting to see which brand I select. If I decide on yours, I'll give you their names."

You'll profit if, *at the beginning* of your sales presentation, you'll say something like this: "Mr. Adams, our firm wants us to ask you a question before we start our sales presentation. They've found that if we wait until the end we frequently forget to ask it. Here's the question: Can you let me have the names of some other people who are interested in installing air conditioning?"

Even though you may have asked for—and obtained—some prospects at the *beginning* of your presentation, it's a good idea to ask for prospects again at the *end* of your presentation. This is true even if you haven't closed the order. The original prospect may have thought up some names by then.

Good results are often obtained by asking, "Do you know anyone else who is considering buying a [whatever your product may be]?"

In addition, be sure to ask a question like the following, according to what your product is:

"Do you know anyone else who still shovels coal?" "Are there any elderly people, or people in poor health, around here?"

"Do you know of anyone who works all day in an air-conditioned office and then comes home at night to a hot, humid house?"

"Do you know any young couples who have small children whom they'd like to send to college some day?"

"Have some of your friends or neighbors cars that look as if they should be replaced?"

Users or owners are a productive source of suspects, or even prospects, when properly approached. (While users of your own brand of merchandise are preferable, don't bypass users of the same type of merchandise, even if not your brand. Names of prospects can be obtained from them too.) When you call on users of your own product for names of new prospects, don't ask them how they like your equipment. If you do, you may bring in many service calls instead of acquiring prospects. This isn't condemning your product. No matter how good it may be, human nature is such that, if asked, people can always find something wrong.

Come straight to the point: "Mrs. Baker, some of your friends or relatives or neighbors must have seen your new automatic laundry drier. I wonder if you would give me the names of those who appeared to be most interested. I won't use your name unless you say so."

Of course, if the customer volunteers a complaint, handle it graciously and promptly. In such cases it's a good idea to telephone your service department from the customer's home, where this is practicable and agreeable to the customer. This action usually pleases her. Moreover, in her presence you can make an appointment with the service department that is convenient for her.

In most fields, ten user calls a day will keep you provided with high-grade suspects if you ask the right questions in the right way. You can then follow up these suspects and convert a good percentage of them into prospects. And you can develop the prospects so as to produce a satisfactory volume of sales.

EXPLORE ALL SOURCES OF PROSPECTS

There are other sources of prospects in addition to users. Newspapers, with their accounts of births, deaths, wills probated, promotions, real estate transfers, building permits issued, fires, burglaries, accidents, etc., provide a steady flow of suspects to salesmen in various fields of endeavor. Reports from such agencies as Dodge, Dun & Bradstreet, and *The Legal Intelligencer* are also helpful. If you read the classified telephone directory you may find a group of companies who might be logical "suspects" for your merchandise. Lists of automobile registrations have been used to good advantage by automobile salesmen.

Productive salesmen are careful to find out what line of business their friends are following and are equally careful that these friends are acquainted with their own endeavors. "I'll keep my eyes and ears open and pass on to you anything in your field," they say, "and I know you'll do the same for me." They also try to get companies in allied lines to work with them. Salesmen of home appliances, for example, try to arrange contacts with real estate offices.

Keep alert for new uses for your merchandise and new types of customers for it. Frequently these new uses are developed by the customers. The new type of prospect often comes to the salesman, instead of the salesman's going after that original prospect. In such cases as this, the salesman may not have even a suspicion that this type of potential user might be interested in his product.

Prospects may come from an unexpected source. A classic

example of this is the white goods converter who was approached some thirty-odd years ago by a tea merchant, to see if white muslin could be produced sufficiently free of bleaching chemicals and sizing to be used as tea bags. As soon as the problem was solved, the converter's salesmen approached other tea merchants with the idea, and sold them. Thus an important amount of yardage from a new and unsuspected source was added to the white goods market.

Conversely, the supplanting of fabric tea bags by today's parchment bags originated not with the tea merchants but with the parchment manufacturers.

USE THE TELEPHONE WISELY FOR PROSPECTING

Bear in mind that one of your best sales weapons is *you*. Over the telephone, this strange new prospect doesn't know whether you're a crook, a thug, or a bum. When he sees you in person, your appearance is helping sell YOU. At a glance, he determines that you're neat and gentlemanly and sober—not a bad guy at all. Thus one doubt and its attendant handicap are quickly eliminated from his mind.

Therefore, when you receive a recommendation or suggestion to call on a brand-new prospect who may not be expecting you, if it's practicable call on him in person instead of using the telephone to make the appointment for a sales interview.

Billions of dollars of merchandise have been sold over the telephone. Expert salesmen know when to use it for selling. Without it modern business would be greatly restricted. Yet, used improperly or on unsuitable merchandise, the telephone can lose sales rather than gain them for you.

- Certain types of selling are ideally suited for use of the telephone, such as selling of merchandise that is either *staple* or so *well known* that it needs no description to the prospect or customer. Here are some telephone prospecting sales stories:

"Jim, I've some good news for you. You're one of our good customers I'm telephoning to give a chance at this. You know how short of high-temperature quelching oil everybody has been? Well, we've just received notice that we'll have a limited amount on Thursday. Would you be interested in getting a little of it?"

"Bob, we understand that, because of the steel strike, prices
160

on our equipment will shortly advance. We still have a few Model 145's on hand that are available at the old price. We wonder if you'd want to cover yourself on a few before the price advances?"

Another desirable field for telephone selling is your list of *established customers*. You know them and their needs, and they know you. If you have something, as above, that's either in short supply or particularly attractively priced, you'll find the telephone a great help in swelling your sales volume.

An important requirement for telephone selling is that no customer signature be needed on the order, unless it's practically automatic with him. For example, the buyer for a department store will tell you over the telephone, "You may ship me twenty dozen. My confirming order will be in the mail tonight. The order number is B6155."

On the contrary, if you're trying to sell a specialty, or if there's financing involved so that your printed order must be signed, such a situation doesn't lend itself to telephone selling. Over the telephone, how are you going to put the order in front of the prospect at the crucial moment, when you've brought him up to the boiling point? Won't you be taking a chance that he'll cool off by the time you arrive with the order for his signature?

Don't attempt, on the telephone, selling requiring involved or lengthy explanations of technical points. You lose the opportunity of simplifying and expediting your sale with pictures, diagrams, manuals, and models. Over the telephone it's difficult for you to explain, and for your prospect to understand, the points you're hoping to emphasize.

Don't try to sell on the telephone where two signatures are involved, such as those of husband and wife. You may think you've gotten one of them on your team, only to find on a follow-up personal interview that the running mate has pulled the first one off.

In situations such as the above, where use of the telephone is not ideal for actual selling, it can still be utilized for various types of canvassing, for making appointments (as explained previously), and—in cases where it appears advisable—for prospect "warming." This applies to those whom you've previously called, without selling them.

Here are some examples of prospect "warming":

"Mr. King, would it be convenient for you to see me for a few minutes either this afternoon or tomorrow morning? I've just gotten hold of a wonderful buy for you."

"Mr. Mann, when I call on you tomorrow afternoon, I'll have something very interesting for you to see."

"Mr. Landis, I think we've licked the biggest problem in your installation. I'll tell you about it when I see you on Wednesday."

The important thing to remember about the telephone is to use it in the right way, on the right merchandise, and on the right kind of prospect.

ENCOURAGE YOUR CUSTOMERS
TO PROSPECT FOR YOU

George M. Dodson suggests the following ideas for getting the cooperation of customers to prospect for you:

"*Most important* point in making a sale is to prove to the customer that your product or line meets his own needs satisfactorily. He will no doubt tell that much, if anyone asks him. But if you want him to open discussions with other prospects, give him an additional fact or two about which he can brag a bit! Customers enjoy talking about why their purchase is not only good but really the very best.

"*Be sure* your customers know where to reach you quickly when they uncover a prospect or have a sale well along the way for you. Lots of people show almost no initiative in locating names and addresses. So furnish sufficient printed material at frequent intervals to allow customers to end a discussion with the statement, 'Here is the address and phone number of the salesman from whom I bought.' "*

You Are Now Ready to Think of Additional Ways to Get Prospects

The above methods by no means exhaust the sources of prospects. There are many more, varying, of course, from industry to industry. You can think of several additional ways of getting prospects for your own product.

* George M. Dodson, "How to Let Your Customers Help," *Specialty Salesman*, November 1957, p. 54.

If you say, "I haven't any prospects," this means either that you aren't making the necessary number of prospecting calls or, if you are making plenty of prospecting calls, that you aren't handling them properly. It's a confession by you that you aren't putting forth the right amount of effort, in the right way, to get prospects.

KEY REVIEW POINTS FOR SELF-IMPROVEMENT

What must you have before you make a sale?

Why should you add new prospects to your list, even where you have an established clientele?

Name three ways of finding prospects.

What method or methods of obtaining prospects have you found particularly productive?

What methods are you using now?

At what points during a sales presentation should you ask for prospects?

When is another time during the sales presentation that you may be able to pick up prospects?

Who are "suspects" for your particular merchandise?

How can you go about making up a list of such suspects?

**The first step toward failure
is to stop prospecting**

Chapter 13

Increasing Your Earnings

Have a **plan** and **use** it; don't **discard, examine**
  it; **pre**-pare; set up a **work pattern**
Spend your time for **your benefit: with** prospects,
  selling not servicing, for **payoff** calls
Help your product **resell**
Straight-line selling
Expect to get the **order**
Don't accept **defeat**
Special reminders to **increase your sales**

WHILE SOME salesmen have innate ability, their selling activities
are not organized. Some salesmen don't exert any more effort
than is required to yield them a comfortable living. It's amazing how many salesmen spend two or three weekdays each
week playing golf! So many such salesmen aren't too hard to
surpass if you'll use method in arranging your work and actually put forth conscientious and intelligent effort.

Plan Your Sales Effort

First of all, *plan* your prospecting, your selling, and your
personal activities. Then work your plan.

It's a good idea to write on paper your sales promotion campaign for the entire year, month by month. Carefully file away
these valuable sheets of paper. Without this record, twelve
months from now you may have forgotten what particular
effort or development helped produce a given month's healthy
volume.

EXAMINE SALES STRATEGIES BEFORE
DISCARDING THEM

Should you try a particular idea and find it ineffective, it's
not unwise to discard it. Before you abandon it, however,

examine it thoroughly. Make sure that each word is carefully chosen to produce the best results. Sometimes a slight change can make a previously limping idea spurt briskly. *Don't give up* a plan or idea until you're sure that you've given it a thorough trial, and you're sure that you've used it in the most effective manner possible.

Planned sales stories have been the basis of the most effective selling campaigns and of many of the most successful companies. You're urged again to construct a planned selling story, and to use it. This is covered in Chapter 3. It might be well to reread that chapter at this point if you want to review its suggestions.

In the present chapter you'll be reminded of the necessity of making calls and of remaining in the presence of prospects. These activities, as well as the handling of your personal affairs, should be so planned by you that you will work as efficiently as you possibly can.

PRE-PREPARE FOR EACH SALES CALL

Several steps should be taken before making a sales presentation. One is to make yourself familiar with the selling points of your product and with the literature and manuals covering it, so that you can quickly find the booklet and the pages in it that answer probable questions of prospects. Even where you know all the selling points of your product, your strongest presentation is backed up with actual demonstration or with pictures or with the printed word—or with all three of these.

You should prepare your sales story—if not word for word, certainly in outline form—so that you know what your selling plan will be. Be sure to have a supply of order forms, finance papers, literature, and demonstration samples so organized that you can find any such material when you need it.

Know what you're going to do each day of each week and each hour of each day. If you leave your daily activities to chance, the results will likewise be a matter of chance.

AVOID SHORT CUTS AND FALLACIES

In selling, as in other endeavors, the *surest short cut to success is hard work*. New salesmen in particular have a tendency to bubble over with short cuts, such as: "Making calls to find prospects takes a lot of time. I could spend this time to better advantage on selling. I'm a salesman, not a canvasser." Other such fallacies are as follows:

"All we need to do to get prospects is to run some good, strong newspaper advertising."

"Let's send out direct-mail, return-prepaid post cards."

"How about some house-to-house circulars? Hang 'em on the doorknobs and have return post cards with 'em."

"Let's have a central city location and people will rush right in to buy our product."

"Hire a girl and put her on a telephone canvass. She'll dig up lots of prospects."

Those are just a few samples of the suggestions. Each one has merit. All of them have been productive. But the point that the suggester completely overlooks is that these ideas are to be used *in addition to* solid effort by the salesman in finding his own prospects. Ideas such as the above are *adjuncts* to personal effort, *not substitutes* for it. Used alone, and without prospecting activity on the part of the salesman, these promotions normally become so costly as to be prohibitive.

(At this point, you're reminded to once more check the specific methods of obtaining prospects given in Chapter 12.)

SET UP A WORK PATTERN FOR YOURSELF

Set a minimum number of sales presentations for a week, for a month, and for a year. The number of productive calls will vary, depending upon the product or service sold and the type of customer called on. The Canada Dry sales-service representative, for example, is reputed to make 70 sales-service calls a DAY. In a five-day week this would amount to 350 calls. At the other extreme, an active diesel locomotive sales engineer might well be highly successful and productive if he were fortunate enough to make one original sales presentation per week (as distinguished from a follow-up) the year round.

Bertrand R. Canfield suggests the following five steps to salesmen for systematizing activities for more profitable sales results: *

1. Set daily activity quotas
2. Schedule daily calls and interviews

* Bertrand R. Canfield, *Salesmanship Practices and Problems*, New York: McGraw-Hill, 1958, p. 345.

3. Keep records of daily, weekly, and monthly sales performance

4. Review and analyze each day's work

5. Plan next day's work.

Considering the problems of the men who sell real estate, insurance, automobiles, air conditioning, investments, automatic heating, insulation, storm windows, roofing and siding, and similar products—eighteen sales presentations a week, to true prospects, should give these men a generous income. If you're in a classification similar to the above and don't sell enough from eighteen sales presentations a week, then either you're calling on the wrong people or you're giving your sales presentation in the wrong manner. Careful study of this book will do much to help you solve your problem.

Your Time Is Important

ARRANGE TO SPEND MORE TIME IN THE PRESENCE OF PROSPECTS

One of your problems is to arrange your activities so that you can spend *most of your time in the presence of prospects* —people who are actually interested in your product. To be successful, you should show up at the office not oftener than one afternoon a week, and only for an hour or two. And this should be when you're scheduled to do so, for meetings or for meeting customers there.

You can turn in complaints by telephone or by a brief note. Write your reports at times when you wouldn't be seeing a prospect, and mail them to the office. Canvass for new prospects at a time when most prospects find it unsatisfactory to hear a complete sales demonstration. For example, canvassing for leads for such products as storm windows and insulating materials is usually best during the daytime. Since the sale ordinarily must be made to both husband and wife, the evenings and Saturdays (and sometimes Sundays and holidays) are reserved for sales activities.

If you're a specialty salesman and are selling home appliances, where husband and wife both must be sold, you'll be wise to attempt to schedule as many sales presentations as possible during the daytime with retired people, men on night

167

work, men on vacation, widows and spinsters, etc. This will enable you to hold your evenings open for prospects whom you can see at no other time.

DON'T BECOME A SERVICE MAN—
YOU'RE A SALESMAN

Even where you know you can't get any repeat business at the moment, it's usually advisable to allot a limited amount of your time to calling on existing customers, to see that they're obtaining maximum results from your product. However, don't spend the majority of your working hours in this endeavor. As a rule, you're paid to be not a service man but a salesman. Plan to spend most of your time in *getting orders*. Arrange to have the service department take over mechanical and technical problems, so that you can devote most of your time to your prime function—selling.

ALLOCATE YOUR TIME AGAINST POTENTIAL
SALES POSSIBILITIES

If you're selling a repeat product, your accounting department will give you a list of your customers showing the percentage of your volume that each customer provides. Then you can make tests to see whether it pays you best to spend 40 per cent of your time with the 40 per cent customer and 2 per cent of your time with the 2 per cent customer. Or perhaps some of the 1 per cent and 2 per cent customers can be developed by effort and time spent by you.

It's evident that the more calls you make, the more sales you'll close, isn't it? Have you ever seen a new man make a few calls without closing a sale, then decide that selling isn't for him? Or have you seen him make three prospect calls a day for three days without obtaining an order? Often he gives up in disgust at this point, because he feels that he's in the wrong business.

Before this happens to you, consider that probably two factors are askew in the above situation. First, you have to use the proper technique to be successful in selling. Second, you have to make plenty of such calls in effective selling.

MAKE CALLS—BUT MAKE THEM PAYOFF CALLS

If you're a house-to-house salesman and you ring a hundred

doorbells in a day and find two homes where the owner is sufficiently interested to permit you to give a complete sales demonstration to husband and wife together, you have, to be sure, rung a hundred doorbells. But you've made *only two selling calls*. And it's these selling calls that are the payoff calls.

"The more payoff calls, the more sales" is a statement so obvious and so fundamental that it appears to require no amplification. Yet, if you're not careful, you'll find yourself as a salesman putting in several days of "work" each week at the office or elsewhere on routine activities. These may include telephoning, writing letters, filling out reports, and conferring with executives of the company in regard to new products, or even handling customer complaints. When the end of the week arrives, if you're one of these misguided individuals, you'll find you've had a zero production in sales. Oh, yes, you've called on prospects, too! You've managed to squeeze into your crowded calendar during the week the total sum of THREE calls on prospects. And each of these prospects proved to be a dud. So no sales resulted.

Don't kid yourself! Make calls—*but payoff calls* and plenty of them—if you want to make sales.

Help Your Customers to Resell More Profitably

If you're selling a product to customers who in turn sell it, be sure to spend some of your time in helping your customers sell more of *your* product to *their* customers. (In some companies, the sales promotion department takes care of this activity, but even then salesmen must coordinate all such activities with an account.)

HOW MANUFACTURERS' SALESMEN CAN HELP RESALE SALESMEN

If you are employed by a manufacturer to sell appliances to wholesale distributors, these wholesale distributors sell in turn to retail stores. Finally, these stores sell the appliances to the ultimate consumer. In five basic ways you can help your distributors to increase their sales of your appliances:

1. *You can* keep them informed of advertising and promotional campaigns used successfully by other distributors of your product.

2. *You can* accompany distributors' salesmen during their calls on some of their retail store customers

    a. and lend the distributors' salesmen a *helping hand* in actual sales presentations where they have extraordinarily tough market conditions;

    b. and observe the selling technique of your distributors' salesmen to see if you can *suggest ideas* that will improve their volume.

3. *You can* be sure that the wholesale distributors' salesmen are helping the salesmen of their retail store accounts in the same manner that you assist the wholesalers' salesmen. In addition, if the latter will accompany you without objections, at times you can gain by giving help to the retail salesman who has a particularly difficult prospect.

4. *You may,* with the approval and cooperation of your distributors' sales departments, also hold sales meetings for their customers' salesmen.

5. *You can* initiate sales contests for your distributors' salesmen and for the salesmen of their retail outlets.

In some companies, activities such as the above are functions of the sales promotion and advertising departments.

With a little thought, you can develop other methods of increasing your volume by helping your customers increase *their* volume. The above is intended to be illustrative, not complete.

Strive to Sell the Straight-Line Way

When you give your sales presentation, hew to the line; keep to the subject, use straight-line selling.

You'll recall that in Chapter 3 you saw a picture of a sale. You remember that you're trying to take the prospect upward from 32° to 212° (from freezing to boiling), and that when you get him to the boiling point you put the order in front of him for his signature.

Many prospects, either intentionally or accidentally, draw the salesman away from his set course. Some salesmen, without realizing it and without meaning to do so, pull *themselves* away from their planned progress. In either case, the results are similar.

When you've wandered from your subject several times, even if you finally finish your sales presentation, your prospect rarely reaches the same buying temperature as if you'd kept him on the planned course. Why? Because his mind has been filled and diverted with random bits of information and disturbing ideas. These are mingling with the sales features you've managed to include. Frequently they dull your points. Sometimes they distort them. Many times they obscure them.

Straight-line selling means a well-organized sales story consisting of major selling points. After each major point, you try for at least three commitments. Each point so handled should raise the prospect's buying temperature. Thus he progressively moves in a straight line upward toward the closing point.

CORRECT HANDLING OF INTERRUPTIONS

What you should do when, during your carefully organized presentation, the prospect throws questions at you that are foreign to the points you're trying to make? If you answer them with the explanation they require, you'll wander miles away from the particular subject you're trying to cover. If you don't answer them, you leave a doubt in his mind and he continues to think of his disturbing question instead of listening and following your explanation.

Such interruptions are bound to have a disrupting effect on your sales presentation, no matter how you handle them. However, you can minimize them by the following steps:

1. *Stop* your sales presentation TEMPORARILY.

2. *Rephrase* the prospect's question in your own words (so that he'll be sure that you understand what's in his mind).

3. *Answer* him Yes or No as briefly as is polite. Something like this might do: "No, Mr. Platt, that can't happen with our product."

4. *Tell him* his point will be covered. For example: "If you don't mind waiting, I have planned to cover this point a little later on in our interview." (Be sure to keep this promise at a convenient spot as your presentation unfolds, if he seems to require an extended explanation.)

5. *Write his question* on your pad, and inform him that you're doing this so you'll be sure not to forget it later on.

6. *Obtain his agreement* to proceed, and then briefly review before continuing with your planned sales presentation.

171

Assume You Will Make the Sale

During every sales presentation, you should assume in your own thinking that you will obtain the order. After all, you have a good product or good service, haven't you? The prospect has a need for it, hasn't he? You'll tell a good story and try for plenty of commitments, won't you? The prospect is a reasonably intelligent man, isn't he, so that he can understand what you say? You won't forget to try often for the close, will you? So why shouldn't you get the order?

Moreover, in your attitude toward the prospect and in your sales presentation you should convey the idea that you expect his order. Don't talk about "*If* you purchase this equipment." Instead, say, "*When* you have this equipment." Converse with your prospect on the basis of conferring with a future happy owner, who will enjoy the benefits that your product will bring him.

Don't Assume Defeat

REALIZE A PROSPECT'S NO DOESN'T ALWAYS MEAN NO

While you're giving your sales presentation, you'll hear many No's from the prospect. Don't accept them without knowing what the prospect means by the No! Let's assume that you've tried six times for the order. Let's further assume that in each case the prospect has said No. The sixth No! is much weaker than the first one. Of course, it sounds stronger and louder to you—and perhaps the prospect has shouted it more loudly. Actually, however, from a psychological point of view his last No may be weaker than the first one. After all, haven't you been giving him additional reasons why he should have your product? And shouldn't these reasons be helping you to soften his attitude?

To be extreme, we might say that if you obtain sixteen No's and one final Yes, you'll have accomplished what you set out to do. You'll have helped the prospect to become a customer.

USE THE "I DON'T BELIEVE" TECHNIQUE

Some prospects who say No will respond favorably to the "I don't believe" technique. This may be used where the prospect has said No quite emphatically.

You reply, "I believe you when you say No, Mr. Quinn, but *I don't believe* you mean what you say. You're too thoughtful and considerate to mean 'No, I don't want to relieve my wife of disagreeable drudgery.' You're too intelligent to mean 'No, I don't want to modernize my home.' You're too good a technical man to mean 'No, I don't think your exclusive features —your combined heating and cooling unit, your permanent electrostatic filters, and your automatic comfort control—are well-engineered and desirable components in equipment of this type.' Yet, Mr. Quinn, when you say No you're depriving your family and yourself of many advantages and benefits that our year-round air conditioner will bring. I think you really want those advantages and benefits—for your wife if not for yourself. And those advantages and benefits can be assured if you will just put your name right there, Mr. Quinn."

DISTINGUISH BETWEEN A TEMPORARY SETBACK AND DEFEAT

Be sure not to mistake a temporary setback for a permanent defeat. No salesman sells *every* prospect on whom he calls. In some fields a man who can close one sale for every three of his sales presentations makes a comfortable living. The profession of selling requires resilience. Each sale that you lose will help you improve, if you'll check back over your presentation and try to *find out where you were weak* and what you did wrong, and resolve not to make the same mistakes again.

If you've given six sales presentations without a close, don't get downhearted. Assuming that you've been analyzing your procedure and have been taking corrective action, each presentation can well be an improvement over the previous one. The next three can all bring orders—if you go at them the right way.

When you're turned down after a sales presentation, if you're weak you'll consider it a lost cause. But before crossing such a prospect off your list, check carefully to determine whether or not you're mistaking a temporary setback for a permanent defeat. Ask yourself, "Did I handle the presentation properly?"

Special Reminders for You to Remember

MAKE A CHECK-UP—FOR FOLLOW-UP CALLS

Go over it mentally, step by step. If at any place you can strengthen your sales-interviewing technique by new information or inducements that you can offer, present them, together with your improvements and other additions, on your follow-up call or calls. Be sure to include answers to these questions in your check-up:

1. Did I tell a good story?
2. Did I tell it in the right way?
3. Did I get plenty of commitments?
4. When did I try for the close?
5. What did I do wrong?
6. What did I omit?
7. Did I antagonize the prospect?

USE LANGUAGE THE PROSPECT UNDERSTANDS

It's wise to use simple language in your sales presentations —the simpler the better. Some salesmen know their product so thoroughly that they use language too technical for the prospect to understand. "Dehumidification" and "a psychometric chart" may be elementary to the air-conditioning salesman, but it's always advisable to add some words of simple explanation even when talking to an engineer. Engineers may be specialists in a field different from yours, and therefore they can be unfamiliar with your technical vocabulary.

You don't want to insult any prospect's intelligence, so you should be careful to be diplomatic in your explanations. An expression such as "You know and I know this means . . ." or "Your experience no doubt has been such-and-such with such-and-such" can be used effectively to help solve this problem.

Remember that it isn't *what* you say, it's *how* you say it that lends strength and conviction to your remarks. There's a *best* way of saying anything. That best way includes two factors:

1. *Proper phrasing*—the choice of the most telling words.
2. *Enthusiasm*—if *you're* not enthusiastic about your product, how can you expect to create sufficient enthusiasm in your prospect to move him to buy?

Small changes in phrasing can make a big difference. Have you ever heard a salesman say to his sales manager, "I told the prospect just what you said, but I didn't get the order"?

The chances are that the man is telling the truth—he *did* convey to the prospect the idea suggested by the sales manager.

But did he use the sales manager's exact words? Probably not. A proper choice of words and phrasing cannot be overemphasized. By experimenting, by listening to other salesmen, by studying your product and your sales manual, you can find words and phrases that will produce for you better than other words or expressions. Incorporate such selling words and phrases into your sales presentation.

As an example of careful choice of words, today's life insurance salesmen have been previously mentioned. Those who are successful rarely ask a prospect, "How about some more insurance?" Instead, you'll recall they ask something like this: "Wouldn't you like to find a painless way of providing for your son's college education?"

Another example of the proper choice of words (already described in Chapter 2) occurred with a group of house-to-house canvassers for storm windows. With meager results they were trying as a door-opener: "I'm not here to talk to you now. I just wonder *if* you can spare two minutes to answer a question."

The most common answer to this by the housewife was: "I'm so busy I can't spare even two seconds, let alone two minutes."

By changing the one "if" to "when," this was transformed into the highly successful approach: "I'm not here to talk to you now. I just wonder *when* you can spare two minutes to answer a question."

You'll recall that the most frequent answer to this by the housewife (and she usually had a smile) was, "I guess I can spare two minutes right now. What is the question?"

Guard against words causing prospects to withdraw. In searching for the right phrasing, you should guard against words that cause prospects to withdraw or to put up their guard. Instead, use words that will draw them to you and that will lower their defenses. For example, if you say, "I'll *show* you how and why our product is *years* ahead of any other make," the prospect withdraws and puts up his guard. His mental response is, "So this so-and-so is going to *show* me why his product is the best, is he? I dare him to!"

If, instead of talking about "showing," you say, "I'll let you *see* with your own eyes—and then *you* can be the judge—how and why our product is *years* ahead of any other make," you

175

don't create antagonism. In fact, the prospect is raised in his own estimation and he reaches out to cooperate, to see, and to judge the features you present.

YOUR PEP AND ENTHUSIASM CAN MAKE A BIG DIFFERENCE

No matter how well-chosen the words and the phrasing may be, if the salesman talks in a monotone, without enthusiasm, his presentation is greatly weakened. A salesman telling the same story day after day, week after week, must not lose his enthusiasm. Very quickly it becomes old and familiar—and perhaps even somewhat boring—to him. But to the prospect it's still new. The successful salesman keeps his presentation bright and sparkling, and for each prospect he puts on the best show in his power.

In fact, there's much similarity between the salesman and the star of a theatrical hit who makes the same speeches and movements through hundreds of performances. It's all old stuff to the actor. But to the audience it's new and alive and wonderful. At each performance it's the first time that the audience has seen the show. You must remember, when you give your sales presentation—even for the thousandth time— to *make it shining and exciting to the prospect*. No matter how old and familiar your sales story is to you, it's new and strange and wonderful to him.

ROLL OUT THE RED CARPET FOR THE BUDGET BUYER AS WELL AS THE PROSPEROUS BUYER

Always give a good performance! Never forget to be enthusiastic in your sales presentation if you want your prospect to acquire sufficient interest to develop into a customer. This applies regardless of whether he is interested in the highest-priced or the lowest-priced merchandise in your line. In fact, you won't be wrong if you treat the budget buyer with the same care and consideration as if he were purchasing the finest and most expensive product available.

Suppose, for example, you're a used-car salesman and you've been averaging between $1500 and $2000 per car. A not-too-prosperous-looking prospect comes up to you and asks, "Can

I get an automobile for not over $250, the full price?" If you can fill his requirement, you handle him with the same "roll-out-the-red-rug" treatment that you use on prospects for higher-priced merchandise.

This isn't courtesy alone. It isn't sympathy and understanding alone. It's good business. If he's treated right, he'll come back. Conditions may improve for him. He may become a very desirable customer in his own right. Moreover, he has friends and relatives that he can guide in your direction.

His small purchase may mean much more to him than the dollar value indicates; and, as illustrated above, it can also mean much more to you than the immediate sale. To the majority of buyers who make a purchase of merchandise selling for $100 and up, the occasion is an important event. That coat, or rug, or television set, or freezer, or washing machine, or automobile, or whatever, may be just a part of the day's work for the salesman or saleswoman. But, in most cases, for the prospect the outlay has been a matter of family discussion over a period of time. Perhaps there has been a waiting period of weeks, or even months, until funds were slowly saved for this purchase.

The $250 fifth-hand jalopy that they eye so longingly may be the first car Mr. and Mrs. Yearning have ever owned. It can well be more important to them than is the new Imperial or Cadillac being purchased by Mr. Wealthy to add to his fleet of six other cars of the same make.

If you don't give your prospects the best sales story that you can and the best demonstration in your power, you're dulling the glow of this big occasion. Even Mr. Wealthy enjoys spending money, and even he likes to know the points of superiority of his car and why it's worth the price he paid.

Use Your Time Profitably When Sales Drop

Too many salesmen merely sit around and mope when orders fall off. Don't you be one of them. A decline in sales doesn't always prove you are doing something wrong. Of course you would like to keep your sales on a steady increase, but this is impossible. When business is down, it's a good time to do three things: *First*, make certain your sales are not dropping as much as those of your competitors. Find out how you really stand. *Second,* this is a good opportunity for some self-interrogation. Some of your best ideas and improvements in yourself as a salesman will often come out of such periods. *Third,* set up a program of getting prospects and servicing present customers. One salesman recently said, "When sales got tough, for the first time I realized the importance of taking care of a customer with a complaint."

This chapter has reminded you that intelligent, planned sales effort will pay off in selling. As a salesman, you can't go through motions and expect to make a good income. Don't let temporary turndowns discourage you, but keep trying!

To sell successfully, a smooth-flowing sales presentation is most helpful. Chapter 14 provides a quick review of how to handle various sales situations that arise. The review and use of such suggested solutions will give your sales interview the professional touches that will help make it smooth-flowing to more Yes decisions.

KEY REVIEW POINTS FOR
SELF-IMPROVEMENT

Why should you write down your sales promotion plan for the entire year?

What should you do before you discard an idea that has proven ineffective?

When you sell to customers a product that they in turn resell, how should you spend some of your time?

Why should you use part of your time to call on present customers?

How can your accounting department help you plan your selling activities?

Where should a salesman spend most of his time?

How can he do this?

What preinterview steps should you take before starting out to sell?

What should you know about each day of each week and each hour of each day?

What is the surest short cut to success in selling?

How many sales presentations each week should you make to insure yourself an adequate income?

How many sales should you close each week?

How many calls on new prospects should you make each week?

How many follow-up sales presentations each week should you make on prospects to whom you've previously given your sales demonstration without closing?

How many follow-up calls are justified on a prospect?

How can you arrange your activities so that you spend a higher percentage of your time in the presence of prospects?

How often and how long each week should you be in the office?

What is the advantage of making as many daytime sales presentations, or as many nighttime sales presentations, as possible?

Why should you keep to your subject and to your planned sales routine?

How should you handle diversionary questions the prospect asks?

Describe how you can assume you'll obtain the order.

How should you converse with the prospect?

Decide which is the weakest No, if the prospect has said No several times.

Explain the "I don't believe" technique.

How can you strengthen and improve your sales presentation after each turndown?

Why should you use simple but colorful language?

What two factors are included in the best way of saying anything?

Why should you avoid words that cause the prospect to withdraw?

Can you give an example of a word or words that will pull prospects toward you?

Why should you be enthusiastic?

Why should you keep your sales presentation shining and sparkling as you give it, even for the thousandth time?

Continue to improve:
You will **outsell** competition
You will **increase** your earnings

Chapter 14

Summary Check List of Thought-Provokers to Assist You to Sell More

Point 1. Have a reserve of prospects if you want to continue to make sales (Chap. 12).

Why should you add new prospects to your list, even if you have an established clientele?

What method or methods of finding prospects have you found particularly productive?

Name at least three additional ways of finding prospects.

Point 2. Watch for and actively seek prospects. Ask for them both at the beginning and at the end of the sales presentation (Chap. 12).

At what two points during a sales interview should you ask for prospects?

When is another time during the sales presentation when you may be able to pick up prospects?

Make a list of "suspects" for your particular merchandise or service.

Point 3. Remember the basic outline of a sale (Chap. 3).

Reconstruct in your mind each sale you have made.

What three major things are you trying to do when you are selling?

Point 4. Bring prospects from freezing to boiling while developing a good story and getting commitments (Chap. 3).

List as many reasons as you can think of why anyone should buy your type of product or service. Choose the strongest three reasons from this list.

Write down as many reasons as you can think of why anyone should buy your product or service rather than any competing brand in the same field. Choose the strongest three reasons from this list.

Write down as many reasons as you can think of why anyone should buy your product or service NOW. Choose the strongest three reasons from this list.

Can you see that, except for the appropriate committing questions, you have gathered together the basic outline for your sales presentation?

Point 5. Get more than one commitment typically to make a sale (Chap. 4).

When you're interviewing the "strong, silent" prospect, how do you handle commitments?

How do you handle the prospect who says he'll buy if you provide him with —— (something unusual)?

Point 6. Get commitments by asking questions (Chap. 4).

What's the simplest way to obtain a commitment?

What strong statements have you been making that would be more acceptable to the prospect in the form of questions?

Point 7. Use committing words such as "understand," "like," "appreciate" (not "convince") (Chap. 4).

Make a list of some other committing words in addition to those listed above.

Why is it better not to say, "I'll convince you . . ."?

What's an easy way of changing a *strong statement* into a *committing question*?

Point 8. Bring prospects to the boiling point; then be sure to close (Chap. 5).

Who does the closing, the prospect or the salesman?

Point 9. Recognize the right time to close (Chap. 5).

When is the right time to close?

How can you tell when this time is at hand?

Give some examples of indicators that a prospect is ready to be sold.

Point 10. Don't wait for the prospect to say he will buy (Chap. 5).

When does the prospect make up his mind that he wants your merchandise and is willing to buy it?

Point 11. Try for the order at least the minimum number of times (Chap. 5).

Why should you try for the close a number of times?

What steps should you take if your attempted test close doesn't produce the order?

181

What should you do when the prospect says, "I want some time in which to think this over"? What does he usually mean?

Point 12. Use alternative tested closes (Chap. 5).

Are there any "magic" closing words?

What is the advantage of using alternate closing questions?

When you're selling to more than one prospect at a time, how should you seat them?

Should you direct your sales demonstration to only one member of a team or group of prospects, or to all of them?

Point 13. Use your time profitably when sales drop (Chap. 13).

What courses of action should you take when you have a drop in sales?

Point 14. Don't let your prospects "cool off" (Chap. 5).

If your prospect tends to cool off because of interruptions or time lapse or for other reasons, how can you warm him up again?

Point 15. Maintain selling reserves (Chap. 5).

How can you build and conserve selling reserves?

When should you use your selling reserves?

When may a relatively unimportant feature carry undue weight with a prospect?

Point 16. Try again when you get a brush-off (Chap. 11).

Why should you try again if you don't get the order on the first call?

Why should you try again when you get a brush-off on a prospecting call?

Point 17. Leave way open to get back (Chap. 11).

When a return call (known as a follow-up call) is in order, why should you give a definite reason and a specific program to your prospect for this return call?

Point 18. Review on return calls (Chap. 11).

1. Three reasons for buying merchandise of your type;
2. Three reasons for buying your brand over other makes;
3. Three reasons for buying NOW.

Why should you review these items?

Point 19. Get recommitments on follow-up calls (Chap. 11).

What is the usual purpose of follow-up or return calls?

Point 20. Get out when you have the order (Chap. 5).

Why is it good practice to leave as soon as possible after obtaining the order?

Point 21. Remember, whatever they have is good (Chap. 8).

Should you condemn a prospect's present line of merchandise? What are the reasons?

What is the difference between building the value of your product and knocking a competitive product?

Point 22. Don't mention competition by name (Chap. 8).

Why shouldn't you mention competitive brands by name?

How can you avoid doing this?

Point 23. Ignore competition. Talk your product. Use "You be the judge" approach (Chap. 8).

When a prospect asks what you think of specific competitive equipment, what should you answer?

What's a good reply when a prospect asks, "What brand do you consider second-best?"

Point 24. Assume there is always competition (Chap. 8).

How can you so construct your sales story as to emphasize clearly your brand's points of superiority without mentioning any other makes?

What is the advantage of telling the story of the evolution of your product?

Point 25. Don't make it easy for competition (Chap. 8).

Name three ways you can make it easy for competition.

Can you think of additional ways you can make it easy for competition?

Point 26. Make it hard for competition (Chap. 8).

How can your users' list make it hard for competition?

If you know you're up against lower-priced competition, what are you going to say?

Where your competitor offers a more extensive guaranty than yours, how can you turn this against him?

Point 27. Eliminate competition (Chap. 8).

Define the "only with" method of eliminating competition.

Define the "rather have" method of eliminating competition.

How do you use a visual chart in eliminating competition?

Where your prospect is attracted by impressive competitive literature, what should you do?

Point 28. Steal the thunder of competition and then beat them to the punch (Chap. 8).

How can you steal the thunder from competitive sales presentations?

Give an example of beating competition to the punch.

Point 29. Approach prospects with confidence (Chap. 2).

What question will disarm a prospect whom you want to see but with whom you don't have an appointment?

How can you be sure you know what to say?

How can you know when the time is right to try for the close?

Point 30. Sell yourself by selling your product (Chap. 10).

What is the surest way of selling yourself?

Point 31. Emphasize the positive; eliminate the negative (Chap. 9).

Give an example of emphasizing the positive and eliminating the negative in selling.

When an unpleasant idea must be brought up, what can you do with it to make it acceptable?

Point 32. Sell yourself by selling your company (Chap. 9).

Can you think of sales you have lost by being critical of your company's policies?

Point 33. Assume you're going to get the order (Chap. 13).

Describe how in your thinking you can assume you'll obtain the order.

How should you converse with the prospect?

Point 34. Have a plan and use it (Chap. 13).

Why should you write down your sales promotion plan for the entire year?

What should you do before you discard an idea that has proved ineffective?

When you sell customers a product that they in turn resell, how should you spend some of your time?

Why should you use a portion of your time to call on existing customers?

How can your accounting department help you plan your selling activities?

Point 35. Make more calls and make more sales (Chap. 13).

Where should a salesman spend most of his time?

Point 36. Prepare (Chap. 13).

What steps should you take before starting out to sell?

Point 37. Realize the only shortcut to success is to work hard (Chap. 13).

What hard work will pay off most for you?

Point 38. Set up a minimum number of sales presentations for each week (Chap. 13).

For most products, how many sales presentations a week should a salesman make to ensure an adequate income?

In your own particular field, how many sales presentations a week should you make?

How many sales presentations a week should you make on new prospects?

How many follow-up sales presentations a week should you make on prospects to whom you've previously given your sales demonstration?

Point 39. Spend as much of your time as possible in the presence of prospects (Chap. 13).

How can you arrange your activities so that you can spend most of your time in the presence of prospects?

How often during the week should you be in the office? How long?

Point 40. Hew to the straight line. Keep to your subject— use straight-line selling (Chap. 13).

How should you handle off-the-subject questions from the prospect?

Point 41. Magnify savings and advantages; shrink expenses and costs (Chap. 9).

Give an example of honest and logical magnification of savings.

Give a similar example of shrinking the cost.

Point 42. Don't talk too much (Chap. 10).

How can you read the prospect's mind?

Describe two ways you can limit your own conversation.

After you've found out what the prospect is thinking, what should you do?

Point 43. Use simple language (Chap. 13).

What words in your vocabulary might some of your prospects not understand?

Point 44. It isn't what you say—it's how you say it (Chap. 13).

What two factors are essential to saying something in the best way?

Why should you avoid words that cause the prospect to withdraw?

Can you give an example of a word or words that will draw prospects to you?

Point 45. Use the "claim" vs. "see" technique (Chap. 10).

How can you handle a prospect who says, "Other makes *claim* the same advantage"?

Point 46. Let them see. Demonstrate with models; use actual installation; bring prospects to your showroom or to wherever your product is in operation (Chap. 10).

Why should you let the prospect see your model or demonstrator and actually handle it and work it—if possible?

What are the advantages of taking your prospect to actual installations and showroom displays?

What are the disadvantages?

How can you help instill confidence in the prospect's mind?

Point 47. Inquire before you attack. Find out what the prospect's objections are before you begin your presentation (Chap. 6).

What are the advantages of finding out what objections the prospect holds against your type of product before you start your sales presentation?

How can you uncover objections?

Point 48. Restate a prospect's objections (Chap. 6).

Why should you restate the prospect's objections in your own words?

Is there any danger in so doing?

Point 49. Get prospects to participate (Chap. 6).

How can you get prospects to participate in your sales demonstrations?

Point 50. Encourage prospect to ask questions (Chap. 6).

Give an example of an invitation to the prospect to ask a question.

Why should you encourage him to ask questions?

Point 51. Tell the "bad news" first (Chap. 9).

Why is it better to bring out the "bad news" at the very beginning rather than delay it until the end?

How can you bring your prospect to the boiling point and keep him there?

Point 52. Relate only the truth (Chap. 10).

Should you ever attempt to bluff the prospect?

Why should your answers be brief?

Point 53. Tell the prospect you don't know, if you don't, but that you will find out (Chap. 10).

If he asks you a question to which you don't know the answer, what should you do?

Point 54. Keep on a "you" basis (Chap. 6).

Why should your sales presentation stress "you" and "yours" rather than "me" and "mine"?

Point 55. Make your point, but don't argue (Chap. 6).

Is a sale a debate?

Why shouldn't you argue with a prospect?

When prospects make antagonistic remarks, how can you get them on your team?

Point 56. Don't lose your self-control (Chap. 6).

Why shouldn't you lose your self-control when selling?

Point 57. Don't interrupt (Chap. 6).

What is the disadvantage of interrupting a prospect?

Point 58. Find out what the key objection is and center your attack on that point (Chap. 6).

How can you discover the prospect's key objection?

After you've found the key objection, what should you do?

How can you focus your regular sales demonstration on the key objection?

Point 59. Have your order pad ready at the beginning of a sale (Chap. 9).

When should you have the order pad handy? Why?

Point 60. Use your sales equipment—but with discretion (Chap. 9).

Should you take each prospect through every page of your sales aids?

How should you use your sales helps?

Point 61. Illustrate with paper and pencil (Chap. 9).

How can you use paper and pencil to help you sell?

How can you use paper and pencil in summarizing?

Point 62. Support every price quotation with explanatory conversation to back up the value of your product or service in the prospect's mind (Chap. 7).

What can you say to make a prospect feel that the value received is greater than the money spent?

Point 63. Don't break down the price if more than your own merchandise is involved in the sale (Chap. 7).

Why is it best not to break down the price if more than your own merchandise is involved in the sale?

Point 64. Don't sell—help them buy (Chap. 6).

Why should you adopt the attitude of acting as the prospect's purchasing agent?

How can you help a prospect buy the right merchandise?

Point 65. Use the telephone for making appointments only on direct calls (Chap. 9).

Explain the difference between a direct and an indirect inquiry from a prospect.

What is the advantage of a personal call by you for making an appointment for a sales demonstration?

Point 66. Sell over the telephone only when a face-to-face call is unnecessary (Chap. 12).

What kind of merchandise is suitable for telephone selling?

What kind of prospects can be sold on the telephone?

Point 67. Sell husband and wife together—particularly when both signatures are needed (Chap. 9).

When signatures of both husband and wife are required, why shouldn't you attempt to sell one without the other?

When you can't escape from giving your sales presentation to one half of the husband-wife team, what should you do?

Point 68. Don't smoke (Chap. 9).

What other mannerisms do you have that might be annoying to your prospects?

Point 69. Don't be rushed, be respected (Chap. 9).

How can you answer the prospect who says, "I can give you only three minutes to tell me all about your product"?

If the prospect says, "In ten minutes I have to leave to catch a plane to Chicago," what can you do?

Point 70. Take it easy (Chap. 9).

What is meant by the advice, "Take it easy"?

Point 71. Have a recess if an interview becomes unduly long (Chap. 9).

On what two occasions may it be advisable to have a recess in your sales presentation?

What should you do at the end of a recess during a long sales presentation?

Point 72. Make it easy to sign and hard not to (Chap. 9).

How can you make it easy for the prospect to sign?

Point 73. Don't believe No's (Chap. 13).

Explain the "I don't believe" technique.

Point 74. Don't mistake a temporary setback for a permanent defeat (Chap. 13).

How can you strengthen and improve your sales presentation after each turndown?

Point 75. Use "sales clinchers" to sign more orders (Chap. 9).

Why shouldn't you use "sales clinchers" unless the order can be signed only by their use?

Point 76. Summarize frequently (Chap. 9).

The summary is a strong auxiliary weapon for what part of the sale?

Point 77. Tell the prospect you're there to get an order—if questioned (Chap. 9).

What can you answer if the prospect expresses surprise, or possibly resentment, when you try to close?

Point 78. Take competitive literature and catalogs, if possible (Chap. 9).

When you've closed a sale and are about to leave, why is it desirable to take competitive literature with you, if your customer will let you have it without protest?

Point 79. Check yourself frequently against this list (Chap. 9).

Why should you check yourself frequently against the list of selling suggestions contained in this book?

How long should you continue periodic check-ups?

Point 80. Add to this list.

Do you know some more successful selling strategies to add to this list?

Analyze your **sales strategies** frequently
What you once knew but have **forgotten**
won't help you sell more today

Chapter 15

A Final Word on Stepping up Your Sales Effectiveness

You Benefit Only When You Use What You Have Learned

Now you've read this book. How much of it do you remember? How much have you put into use and how much more can you employ?

Or perhaps you're a sales executive and have used this work to train your sales force, or your dealers or their salesmen, in the fundamentals of professional salesmanship. How much of it do *they* remember?

Unless an individual is a genius or a near-genius, he doesn't absorb the contents of a book such as this by a single reading or by having it explained to him *once*.

Repetition, study, and *review* are necessary if you are to assimilate and use the ideas contained in this book.

Use Key Review Points to Determine Your Weaknesses

Key review points are provided at the end of each of the chapters to assist the individual salesman or sales executive in determining weaknesses in knowledge.

Most people learn by going over a book or subject several times. Then they begin to absorb and apply what has been learned. Now that you've read this book once, you will profit even more by rereading it. You sales executives, have your salesmen, or your dealers or their salesmen, review this book at least twice, shortly after the first reading. Review your answers to the key review points.

Don't forget that once a month for three months after the initial reading of this book, you should recheck yourself, or be rechecked, against the questions at the end of each chapter.

This process should be repeated at the end of the next three months, and after that, every six months for the rest of your active sales career.

To avoid the monotony of the reviews, some sales managers offer prizes for the most nearly correct answers to the test questions. (Remember that there'll be a close correlation between the highest grades and the highest sales producers.) Others cover their reviews by "group discussions" for each of the ten guides. Different salesmen or dealers lead the discussion on each guide. Sometimes panels of three salesmen or dealers are formed to lead these discussion groups.

Have a "Swap" Session

Some sales managers construct their planned sales story in a "swap shop," where their salesmen or dealers exchange ideas. With this contribution and cooperation, not only is the sales manager's work lightened but the salesmen or dealers have a readier acceptance for a planned sales story they have helped construct than for one that is thrust upon them.

Many successful companies give their new salesmen product training and company indoctrination at the factory. Then these new men are assigned to the branch office in which they are to work. Here the senior salesmen take the new men out into the field and show them how to sell by letting them observe actual sales presentations. Such companies will find this book of considerable benefit, if used at the factory in training new salesmen in the basic techniques of selling before being assigned to a branch office. In this manner not only will each salesman be indoctrinated in the same fundamentals of selling, but also the period of his field training will be shortened and he'll be a more productive salesman in less time.

Other ideas will occur to the alert sales manager to help his men absorb the contents of this book and to assist them in being better salesmen.

Individual Self-Development a Must for Sales Success

To the individual who wishes to improve his sales ability and be a better salesman, we say: As you continue working actively in the field with prospects, as you read books on salesmanship, as you attend courses and meetings, and as you listen to other salesmen tell how they won or lost orders, you will learn additional selling techniques from time to time. When you do, add them to the contents of this book.

Prepare Your Own Sales Strategy Idea Book

No claim is made that these pages tell all there is to know about selling. This book has been started for you. It's up to you to finish it!

It is now up to **YOU**—
You are ready to outsell born salesmen!